YOUR
HO

2008

SCORPIO

YOUR PERSONAL
HOROSCOPE
2008

SCORPIO
24th October–22nd November

igloo

igloo

This edition published by Igloo Books Ltd,
Cottage Farm, Mears Ashby Road, Sywell, Northants NN6 0BJ
www.igloo-books.com
E-mail: Info@igloo-books.com

Produced for Igloo Books by W. Foulsham & Co. Ltd,
The Publishing House, Bennetts Close, Cippenham,
Slough, Berkshire SL1 5AP, England

ISBN: 978-1-845-61614-4

This is an abridged version of material
originally published in *Old Moore's Horoscope
and Astral Diary*.

Printed in China

CONTENTS

INTRODUCTION

Your Personal Horoscopes have been specifically created to allow you to get the most from astrological patterns and the way they have a bearing on not only your zodiac sign, but nuances within it. Using the diary section of the book you can read about the influences and possibilities of each and every day of the year. It will be possible for you to see when you are likely to be cheerful and happy or those times when your nature is in retreat and you will be more circumspect. The diary will help to give you a feel for the specific 'cycles' of astrology and the way they can subtly change your day-to-day life. For example, when you see the sign ☿, this means that the planet Mercury is retrograde at that time. Retrograde means it appears to be running backwards through the zodiac. Such a happening has a significant effect on communication skills, but this is only one small aspect of how the Personal Horoscope can help you.

With Your Personal Horoscope the story doesn't end with the diary pages. It includes simple ways for you to work out the zodiac sign the Moon occupied at the time of your birth, and what this means for your personality. In addition, if you know the time of day you were born, it is possible to discover your Ascendant, yet another important guide to your personal make-up and potential.

Many readers are interested in relationships and in knowing how well they get on with people of other astrological signs. You might also be interested in the way you appear to very different sorts of individuals. If you are such a person, the section on Venus will be of particular interest. Despite the rapidly changing position of this planet, you can work out your Venus sign, and learn what bearing it will have on your life.

Using Your Personal Horoscope you can travel on one of the most fascinating and rewarding journeys that anyone can take – the journey to a better realisation of self.

THE ESSENCE OF SCORPIO

Exploring the Personality of Scorpio the Scorpion

(24TH OCTOBER – 22ND NOVEMBER)

What's in a sign?

To say that you are a little complicated and somewhat difficult to understand is probably a great understatement. The basic reason for this lies in the peculiar nature of Scorpio rulership. In terms of the elements, your zodiac sign is a Water sign. This makes you naturally emotional, deep, somewhat reserved and ever anxious to help those around you. As a direct contrast, classical astrologers always maintained that your planetary ruler was Mars. Mars is the planet of combat and aggression, being positive and dominant under most circumstances. So it can be judged from the start that there are great contradictions within the basic Scorpio nature.

It's a fact that many people are naturally cautious of Scorpio people. Perhaps this isn't surprising. Under most circumstances you appear to be quiet and peaceful, but the situation is a little like a smoking bomb. When it comes to defending yourself, or in particular those people who you see as being important to you, there is virtually no limit to which you would refuse to go. Generally speaking our ancient ancestors were extremely wise in terms of the names they gave to the different zodiac signs. Consider the apparently diminutive and retiring scorpion. It doesn't go looking for trouble and is generally happy to remain in the shadows. However, if it is provoked, or even attacked, it will take on adversaries many times its own size. It carries a barbed sting in its tail and will strike without any additional warning if necessary.

All the same, the Scorpio reputation may be a little undeserved. Yours is one of the most compassionate and caring of all the zodiac signs. When it comes to working on behalf of humanity, especially the oppressed, the sick or the disenfranchised, you show your true mettle. You cannot stand the thought of people suffering unjustifiably, which is why many of the great social reformers and even freedom fighters had the same zodiac sign as you do.

As a Scorpio you are likely to be intuitive (some would say psychic) and under most circumstances you are more than willing to follow that little voice inside yourself that tells you how to behave in any given situation.

Scorpio resources

Your nature is so very often understated that it might be said that your greatest resource is surprise. You have the ability to shock people constantly, even those who think they understand you perfectly well. This brings us back to the creature for which your zodiac sign is named. A scorpion is diminutive – and would represent a tasty snack for any would-be predator. However, it defies logic by standing its ground and fighting back. When it does, woe betide the aggressor that refuses to take account of its presence. And so it is with you. Quiet, even reserved, you tend to get on with your work. This you do efficiently and without undue fuss, approaching each task with the same methodical attitude. People often don't even realise that you are around. And then, when they least expect it, there you are!

The ability to surprise means that you often get on in life against heavy odds. In addition you have great resilience and fortitude. It is possible for you to continue to work long and hard under circumstances that would force others to retreat. Most Scorpio people would not consider themselves to be tough – in fact quite a few are positively neurotic when it comes to matters associated with their own health. Yet you can endure hardship well and almost always win through in the end.

It's true that you may not be quite as confident as you could be. If you were, people would notice you more and that would detract from that all-important element of surprise that makes you so formidable, and which is definitely the most important weapon in your armoury. However, it is clear that your greatest resource is compassion, and on those occasions when you really allow it to show, you display yourself as being one of the most important allies to your fellow men and women.

At a practical level you are more than capable and can often be expected to perform tasks that you haven't necessarily undertaken before. You have a deep intelligence and good powers to reason things out. Most important of all is a determination that no other zodiac sign can match.

Beneath the surface

This section of an account of the typical Scorpio nature could fill an entire book in itself because you are such a complicated person. However, there are certain advantages to being a Scorpio. For example, nobody is going to run away with the idea that you are basically uncomplicated and shallow. It ought to be clear enough to the dullest observer that there is a boiling, seething volcano bubbling away beneath the surface of almost every Scorpio subject.

You are often accused of having a slightly dark view of life, and it's true that many Scorpio people enjoy a rather morbid curiosity and are fascinated by subjects that make other people shudder. At the same time you could hardly be described as being one of life's natural optimists. Part of the reason for this lies in the fact that you have been disappointed in the past and may have arrived at the conclusion that to expect the worst is often the most sensible course of action. At least that way you are likely to mitigate some of the potential depression regarding failures in the future.

Although this way of thinking is somewhat faulty, it comes so naturally to the Scorpio subject that it actually works very well, though it has to be said that it might be responsible for a tendency to hold back on occasions.

Assessing the way your inner mind works is as difficult for you as it is for any outsider. Even individuals who have been friends for years will sometimes come desperately unstuck if they arrive at the conclusion that they know well what makes you tick. In the recesses of your mind you are passionate, driving, restless, dissatisfied and frequently disappointed with your own efforts. On the other hand, you have the power to make dreams into realities and are excellent at hatching plans that will benefit people far from your own circle and circumstances. Being a tireless worker on behalf of the oppressed, the fate of humanity as a whole is ever an inner concern.

When you love you do so with great width and depth. Your capacity for jealousy knows no bounds and there are times when you can be as destructive to yourself as you ever could be regarding any other individual. Yet for all this your inner mind is lofty and can soar like an eagle on occasions. If the world at large was able to fathom just one tenth of the way your inner mind actually works, people would find you even more fascinating than they do already. But perhaps it's best that they don't. The deepest recesses of Scorpio are an intense secret and will usually stay that way.

Making the best of yourself

It isn't hard to find a single word that describes the way you can make the best of yourself, especially when viewed by the world at large. That word is 'communication'. When difficulties arise in your life, especially concerning other people, it's usually because you haven't managed to get your message across, and probably because you haven't even tried to do so. There is much to your nature that is electric, powerful and magnetic. These qualities make you potentially popular and fascinating to a wealth of individuals. Hide these qualities beneath too brusque an exterior and you can seem dark and brooding.

Of course it's a fine line and one that isn't easy to walk. You are constantly worried that if you show people what really makes you tick, they will not find you interesting at all. In reality this concern is totally without foundation. There is more than enough depth about you to last several lifetimes. It doesn't matter how much you give of yourself to the world at large, there are always going to be surprises galore to follow.

Use the dynamic qualities of your nature to the full. Traditionally your ruling planet is Mars – a real go-getter of a planetary ruler and one that imbues you with tremendous power to get things done at a practical level. On the way you need to show how much you care about others. Amidst a plethora of gifts offered to you by the celestial spheres, your ability to help others is likely to be top of the list. When you are giving you are also usually approachable. For you the two go hand in hand. Avoid allowing yourself to become morose or inward looking and always strive to find simple answers to simple questions.

Stick to some sort of work that you find interesting. That can be almost anything to a Scorpio, as long as it feeds the inner you. It does need to carry a degree of diversity and should ideally have an end product that is easy to see. On your journey through life don't get carried away with daydreams – yet on the other hand avoid losing your great potential to make them come true.

The impressions you give

This is one area of your life over which you do have a great deal of control. If the adage 'what you see is what you get' turns out to be true for many signs of the zodiac, it certainly isn't the case with you. The complexity of your nature makes it difficult for even you to find 'the real Scorpio', and in any case this tends to change from day to day. However, regarding some matters there isn't any doubt at all. Firstly you are deeply magnetic and possess the ability to arouse an instinctive fascination in others. Ally this to your propensity for being very positive in your decision making and you have a potentially formidable combination.

Most people already think of you as being an extremely interesting person. Unfortunately they may also occasionally consider you to be a little cool and somewhat difficult to approach. Neither of these impressions are true, it's simply that you are quite shy at heart, and sometimes find it difficult to believe that you could be liked by certain individuals. Learn to throw this erroneous assumption out of the window, and instead, expect to be viewed positively. To do so would make all the difference and would clear the way so that your more personable side can show all the time.

Very few people who know you well could fail to realise that you care deeply, especially about the well-being of the oppressed. You have a truly noble spirit, a fact that shines through in practically everything you do – yet another reason to be noticed.

It's true that you can sometimes make your secretive quality into an art form, which those looking in from the outside might find rather difficult to deal with. This represents another outward aspect of your nature that could so easily be altered. By all means keep your secrets, though not about matters that are of no real note whatsoever. In a single phrase, try to lighten up a little. It's all you need to be almost perfect!

The way forward

It must first be held in mind that Scorpio people are complicated. That's something you simply cannot get away from, no matter how much you might try. On the one hand you can deal with practical matters almost instinctively. You are resourceful, deep thinking, intense and fascinating. On the other side of the coin you are often too fond of luxury and will frequently withdraw yourself from situations that you do not care to pursue. You can be quite stubborn and can even bear a grudge if you feel that you have been provoked. It is suggested in astrology that no quality of nature is necessarily good or bad, it really depends on the way it is used. For example, stubbornness can be considered a terrible fault, but not if you were being awkward concerning the obvious rights of an oppressed person or group. It turns out that Scorpio has more of a potential to be 'saint or sinner' than any zodiac sign. As long as you examine your motives in any given situation, whilst at the same time trying to cultivate a degree of flexibility that is not one of your natural gifts, then you won't go far wrong.

Turn on the charm when it is necessary because it will rarely if ever let you down. Think about the way you can serve the world, but don't preach about it. Love sincerely, but don't allow jealousy to spoil things. Be constructive in your determination and don't get on your high horse when it isn't necessary. Follow these simple rules for the best chance of progress.

Of course there are many positives around to start with. You are a very loyal friend, are capable of being extremely brave and tend to be very committed to family members. At the same time you are trustworthy and can work long and hard using your own initiative. Although you sometimes worry about your health, you are more robust than most and can endure a high degree of hardship if necessary. You don't take kindly to criticism but can be flexible enough to accept it if you know it is intended for your own good.

Few people doubt your sincerity – that is, when they know what you believe. So it's important to lay your thoughts on the line right from the start. And even if you don't choose to treat the whole world as a friend, you are capable of gathering a little circle around you who would never let you down. Do make sure, however, that this 'inner group' isn't simply comprised of other Scorpios!

SCORPIO ON THE CUSP

Astrological profiles are altered for those people born at either the beginning or the end of a zodiac sign, or, more properly, on the cusps of a sign. In the case of Scorpio this would be on the 24th of October and for two or three days after, and similarly at the end of the sign, probably from the 20th to the 22nd of November.

The Libra Cusp – October 24th to 26th

You are probably generally considered to be a bright and breezy sort of character, with a great deal of enthusiasm for life. Despite this, few people would doubt that you are a shrewd operator, and that you know what you want and have a fairly good idea of how to go about getting it. Not everyone likes you as much as you would wish, but that's because the Libran side of your nature longs for popularity, while set against this is your deep Scorpio need to speak your mind, even when you know that other people might wish you did not indulge in this trait very frequently.

In love, you typify the split between these two signs. On the one hand you are passionate, sincere and intense, while on the other your Libran responses can cause a certain fickle sort of affection to show sometimes, probably to the confusion of those with whom you are involved at a personal level. Nevertheless, few people would find fault with your basic nature and there isn't much doubt that your heart is in the right place.

When it comes to career matters, you have a very fortunate combination. Scorpio can sometimes be accused of lacking diplomacy, but nothing could be further from the truth with Libra. As a result, you have what it takes in terms of determination but at the same time you are capable of seeing the point of view put forward by colleagues. You tend to rise to the top of the tree and, with your mixture of raw ability and humour that most of the world approves of, you can stay there.

You won't be the sort of person to make quite as many enemies as Scorpio taken alone might do, and you need the cut and thrust of the world much more than the retiring creature after whom your zodiac sign is named. Try not to be controversial and do your best to retain a sense of humour, which is essential to your well-being. Few would doubt the fact that your heart is in the right place and your creative potential could be second to none. Most important of all, you need the self-satisfaction that comes from living in the real world.

The Sagittarius Cusp – November 20th to 22nd

You can be a really zany character, with a love of life that is second to none. Add to this a penetrating insight, a razor-sharp wit and an instinctive intuition that is quite remarkable and we find in you a formidable person. It's true that not everyone understands what makes you tick, probably least of all yourself, but you strive to be liked and really do want to advertise your willingness to learn and to grow, which isn't always the province of Scorpio when taken alone. Your capacity for work knows no bounds, though you don't really like to get your hands dirty and would feel more content when telling others what to do.

In a career sense, you need to be in a position from which you are able to delegate. This is not because you are afraid of hard work yourself, far from it, but you possess a strong ability to see through problems and you are a natural director of others. Sales careers may interest you, or a position from which you can organise and arrange things. However, you hate to be tied down to one place for long, so you would be at your best when allowed to move around freely and do things in your own way.

You are a natural social reformer, mainly because you are sure that you know what is right and just. In the main you are correct in your assumptions, but there are occasions when you should realise that there is more than one form of truth. Perhaps you are not always quite as patient with certain individuals as you might be but these generally tend to be people who show traits of cruelty or cunning. As a family person, you care very much for the people who figure most prominently in your life. Sometimes you are a definite home bird, with a preference for what you know and love, but this is offset by a restless trend within your nature that often sends you off into the wide blue yonder, chasing rainbows that the Scorpio side of your nature doubts are even there. Few would doubt your charm, your magnetism, or your desire to get ahead in life in almost any way possible. You combine patience with genuine talent and make a loyal, interesting and entertaining friend or lover.

SCORPIO AND ITS ASCENDANTS

The nature of every individual on the planet is composed of the rich variety of zodiac signs and planetary positions that were present at the time of their birth. Your Sun sign, which in your case is Scorpio, is one of the many factors when it comes to assessing the unique person you are. Probably the most important consideration, other than your Sun sign, is to establish the zodiac sign that was rising over the eastern horizon at the time that you were born. This is your Ascending or Rising sign. Most popular astrology fails to take account of the Ascendant, and yet its importance remains with you from the very moment of your birth, through every day of your life. The Ascendant is evident in the way you approach the world, and so, when meeting a person for the first time, it is this astrological influence that you are most likely to notice first. Our Ascending sign essentially represents what we appear to be, while the Sun sign is what we feel inside ourselves.

The Ascendant also has the potential for modifying our overall nature. For example, if you were born at a time of day when Scorpio was passing over the eastern horizon (this would be around the time of dawn) then you would be classed as a double Scorpio. As such, you would typify this zodiac sign, both internally and in your dealings with others. However, if your Ascendant sign turned out to be a Fire sign, such as Aries, there would be a profound alteration of nature, away from the expected qualities of Scorpio.

One of the reasons why popular astrology often ignores the Ascendant is that it has always been rather difficult to establish. We have found a way to make this possible by devising an easy-to-use table, which you will find on page 157 of this book. Using this, you can establish your Ascendant sign at a glance. You will need to know your rough time of birth, then it is simply a case of following the instructions.

For those readers who have no idea of their time of birth it might be worth allowing a good friend, or perhaps your partner, to read through the section that follows this introduction. Someone who deals with you on a regular basis may easily discover your Ascending sign, even though you could have some difficulty establishing it for yourself. A good understanding of this component of your nature is essential if you want to be aware of that 'other person' who is responsible for the way you make contact with the world at large. Your Sun sign, Ascendant sign, and the other pointers in this book will, together, allow you a far better understanding of what makes you tick as an individual. Peeling back the different layers of your astrological make-up can be an enlightening experience, and the Ascendant may represent one of the most important layers of all.

Scorpio with Scorpio Ascendant

This is one of the most potent of all astrological possibilities, but how it is used depends so very much on the individual who possesses it. On the one hand you are magnetic, alluring, sexy, deep and very attractive, whilst at the same time you are capable of being stubborn, self-seeking, vain, over-sensitive and fathomless. It has to be said that under most circumstances the first set of adjectives are the most appropriate, and that is because you keep control of the deeper side, refusing to allow it absolute control over your conscious life. You are able to get almost anything you want from life, but first you have to discover what that might be. The most important factor of all, however, is the way you can offer yourself, totally and without reservation to a needy world.

Self-sacrifice is a marvellous thing, but you can go too far on occasions. The furthest extreme for Scorpios here is a life that is totally dedicated to work and prayer. For the few this is admirable, for the still earth-based, less so. Finding a compromise is not easy as you are not always in touch with yourself. Feed the spiritual, curb the excesses, accept the need for luxury, and be happy.

Scorpio with Sagittarius Ascendant

There are many gains with this combination, and most of you reading this will already be familiar with the majority of them. Sagittarius offers a bright and hopeful approach to life, but may not always have the staying power and the patience to get what it really needs. Scorpio, on the other hand, can be too deep for its own good, is very self-seeking on occasions and extremely giving to others. Both the signs have problems when taken on their own, and, it has to be said, double the difficulties when they come together. But this is not usually the case. Invariably the presence of Scorpio slows down the over-quick responses of the Archer, whilst the inclusion of Sagittarius prevents Scorpio from taking itself too seriously.

Life is so often a game of extremes, when all the great spiritual masters of humanity have indicated that a 'middle way' is the path to choose. You have just the right combination of skills and mental faculties to find that elusive path, and can bring great joy to yourself and others as a result. Most of the time you are happy, optimistic, helpful and a joy to know. You have mental agility, backed up by a stunning intuition, which itself would rarely let you down. Keep a sense of proportion and understand that your depth of intellect is necessary to curb your flighty side.

Scorpio with Capricorn Ascendant

If patience, perseverance and a solid ability to get where you want to go are considered to be the chief components of a happy life, then you should be skipping about every day. Unfortunately this is not always the case and here we have two zodiac signs, both of which can be too deep for their own good. Both Scorpio and Capricorn are inclined to take themselves rather too seriously and your main lesson in life, and some would say the reason you have adopted this zodiac combination, is to 'lighten up'. If all that determination is pushed in the direction of your service to the world at large, you are seen as being one of the kindest people imaginable. This is really the only option for you, because if you turn this tremendous potential power inwards all the time you will become brooding, secretive and sometimes even selfish. Your eyes should be turned towards a needy humanity, which can be served with the dry but definite wit of Capricorn and the true compassion of Scorpio.

It is impossible with this combination to indicate what areas of life suit you the best. Certainly you adore luxury in all its forms, and yet you can get by with almost nothing. You desire travel, and at the same time love the comforts and stability of home. The people who know you best are aware that you are rather special. Listen to what they say.

Scorpio with Aquarius Ascendant

Here we have a combination that shows much promise and a flexibility that allows many changes in direction, allied to a power to succeed, sometimes very much against all the odds. Aquarius lightens the load of the Scorpio mind, turning the depths into potential and making intuitive foresight into a means for getting on in life. There are depths here, because even airy Aquarius isn't too easy to understand, and it is therefore a fact that some people with this combination will always be something of a mystery. However, even this fact can be turned to your advantage because it means that people will always be looking at you. Confidence is so often the key to success in life and the Scorpio–Aquarius mix offers this, or at least appears to do so. Even when this is not entirely the case, the fact that everyone around you believes it to be true is often enough.

You are usually good to know, and show a keen intellect and a deep intelligence, aided by a fascination for life that knows no bounds. When at your best you are giving, understanding, balanced and active. On those occasions when things are not going well for you, beware a stubborn streak and the need to be sensational. Keep it light and happy and you won't go far wrong. Most of you are very, very well loved.

Scorpio with Pisces Ascendant

You stand a chance of disappearing so deep into yourself that other people would need one of those long ladders that cave explorers use, just to find you. It isn't really your fault because both Scorpio and Pisces are Water signs, which are difficult to understand, and you have them both. But that doesn't mean that you should be content to remain in the dark, and the warmth of your nature is all you need to shine a light on the wonderful qualities you possess. But the primary word of warning is that you must put yourself on display and allow others to know what you are, before their appreciation of these facts becomes apparent.

As a server of the world you are second to none and it is hard to find a person with this combination who is not, in some way, looking out for the people around them. Immensely attractive to others, you are also one of the most sought-after lovers. Much of this has to do with your deep and abiding charm, but the air of mystery that surrounds you also helps. Some of you will marry too early, and end up regretting the fact, though the majority of people with Scorpio and Pisces will find the love they deserve in the end. You are able, just, firm but fair, though a sucker for a hard luck story and as kind as the day is long. It's hard to imagine how so many good points could be ignored by others.

Scorpio with Aries Ascendant

The two very different faces of Mars come together in this potent, magnetic and quite awe-inspiring combination. Your natural inclination is towards secrecy, and this fact, together with the natural attractions of the sensual Scorpio nature, makes you the object of great curiosity. This means that you will not go short of attention and should ensure that you are always being analysed by people who may never get to know you at all. At heart you prefer your own company, and yet life appears to find means to push you into the public gaze time and again. Most people with this combination ooze sex appeal and can use this fact as a stepping stone to personal success, yet without losing any integrity or loosening the cords of a deeply moralistic nature.

On those occasions when you do lose your temper, there isn't a character in the length and breadth of the zodiac who would have either the words or the courage to stand against the stream of invective that follows. On really rare occasions you might even scare yourself. A simple look is enough to show family members when you are not amused. Few people are left unmoved by your presence in their life.

Scorpio with Taurus Ascendant

The first, last and most important piece of advice for you is not to take yourself, or anyone else, too seriously. This might be rather a tall order because Scorpio intensifies the deeper qualities of Taurus and can make you rather lacking in the sense of humour that we all need to live our lives in this most imperfect of worlds. You are naturally sensual by nature. This shows itself in a host of ways. In all probability you can spend hours in the bath, love to treat yourself to good food and drink and take your greatest pleasure in neat and orderly surroundings. This can often alienate you from those who live in the same house because other people need to use the bathroom from time to time and they cannot remain tidy indefinitely.

You tend to worry a great deal about things which are really not too important, but don't take this statement too seriously or you will begin to worry about this fact too! You often need to lighten up and should always do your best to tell yourself that most things are not half so important as they seem to be. Be careful over the selection of a life partner and if possible choose someone who is naturally funny and who does not take life anywhere near as seriously as you are inclined to do. At work you are more than capable and in all probability everyone relies heavily on your wise judgements.

Scorpio with Gemini Ascendant

What you are and what you appear to be can be two entirely different things with this combination. Although you appear to be every bit as chatty and even as flighty as Gemini tends to be, nothing could be further from the truth. In reality you have many deep and penetrating insights, all of which are geared towards sorting out potential problems before they come along. Few people would have the ability to pull the wool over your eyes, and you show a much more astute face to the world than is often the case for Gemini taken on its own. The level of your confidence, although not earth-shattering, is much greater with this combination, and you would not be thwarted once you had made up your mind.

There is a slight danger here, however, because Gemini is always inclined to nerve problems of one sort or another. In the main these are slight and fleeting, though the presence of Scorpio can intensify reactions and heighten the possibility of depression, which would not be at all fortunate. The best way round this potential problem is to have a wealth of friends, plenty to do and the sort of variety in your life that suits your Mercury ruler. Financial success is not too difficult to achieve because you can easily earn money and then manage to hold on to it.

Scorpio with Cancer Ascendant

There are few more endearing zodiac combinations than this one. Both signs are Watery in nature and show a desire to work on behalf of humanity as a whole. The world sees you as being genuinely caring, full of sympathy for anyone in trouble and always ready to lend a hand when it is needed. You are a loyal friend, a great supporter of the oppressed and a lover of home and family. In a work sense you are capable, and command respect from your colleagues, even though this comes about courtesy of your quiet competence and not as a result of anything that you might happen to say.

But we should not get too carried away with external factors, or the way that others see you. Inside you are a boiling pool of emotion. You feel more strongly, love more deeply and hurt more fully than any other combination of the Water signs. Even those who think they know you really well would get a shock if they could take a stroll around the deeper recesses of your mind. Although these facts are true, they may be rather beside the point because it is a fact that the truth of your passion, commitment and deep convictions may only surface fully half a dozen times in your life. The fact is that you are a very private person at heart and you don't know how to be any other way.

Scorpio with Leo Ascendant

A Leo with intensity, that's what you are. You are mad about good causes and would argue the hind leg off a donkey in defence of your many ideals. If you are not out there saving the planet you could just be at home in the bath, thinking up the next way to save humanity from its own worst excesses. In your own life, although you love little luxuries, you are sparing and frugal, yet generous as can be to those you take to. It's a fact that you don't like everyone, and of course the same is true in reverse. It might be easier for you to understand why you can dislike than to appreciate the reverse side of the coin, for your pride can be badly dented on occasions. Scorpio brings a tendency to have down spells, though the fact that Leo is also strongly represented in your nature should prevent them from becoming a regular part of your life.

It is important for you to learn how to forgive and forget, and there isn't much point in bearing a grudge because you are basically too noble to do so. If something goes wrong, kiss the situation goodbye and get on with the next interesting adventure, of which there are many in your life. Stop–start situations sometimes get in the way, but there are plenty of people around who would be only too willing to lend a helping hand.

Scorpio with Virgo Ascendant

This is intensity carried through to the absolute. If you have a problem, it is that you fail to externalise all that is going on inside that deep, bubbling cauldron that is your inner self. Realising what you are capable of is not a problem; these only start when you have to make it plain to those around you what you want. Part of the reason for this is that you don't always understand yourself. You love intensely and would do absolutely anything for a person you are fond of, even though you might have to inconvenience yourself a great deal on the way. Relationships can cause you slight problems however, since you need to associate with people who at least come somewhere near to understanding what makes you tick. If you manage to bridge the gap between yourself and the world that constantly knocks on your door, you show yourself to be powerful, magnetic and compulsive.

There are times when you definitely prefer to stay quiet, though you do have a powerful ability to get your message across when you think it is necessary to do so. There are people around who might think that you are a push-over but they could easily get a shock when you sense that the time is right to answer back. You probably have a very orderly house and don't care for clutter of any sort.

Scorpio with Libra Ascendant

There is some tendency for you to be far more deep than the average Libran would appear to be and for this reason it is crucial that you lighten up from time to time. Every person with a Scorpio quality needs to remember that there is a happy and carefree side to all events and your Libran quality should allow you to bear this in mind. Sometimes you try to do too many things at the same time. This is fine if you take the casual overview of Libra, but less sensible when you insist on picking the last bone out of every potential, as is much more the case for Scorpio.

When worries come along, as they sometimes will, be able to listen to what your friends have to say and also realise that they are more than willing to work on your behalf, if only because you are so loyal to them. You do have a quality of self-deception, but this should not get in the way too much if you combine the instinctive actions of Libra with the deep intuition of your Scorpio component.

Probably the most important factor of this combination is your ability to succeed in a financial sense. You make a good manager, but not of the authoritarian sort. Jobs in the media or where you are expected to make up your mind quickly would suit you, because there is always an underpinning of practical sense that rarely lets you down.

29

THE MOON AND THE PART IT PLAYS IN YOUR LIFE

In astrology the Moon is probably the single most important heavenly body after the Sun. Its unique position, as partner to the Earth on its journey around the solar system, means that the Moon appears to pass through the signs of the zodiac extremely quickly. The zodiac position of the Moon at the time of your birth plays a great part in personal character and is especially significant in the build-up of your emotional nature.

Your Own Moon Sign

Discovering the position of the Moon at the time of your birth has always been notoriously difficult because tracking the complex zodiac positions of the Moon is not easy. This process has been reduced to three simple stages with our Lunar Tables. A breakdown of the Moon's zodiac positions can be found from page 35 onwards, so that once you know what your Moon Sign is, you can see what part this plays in the overall build-up of your personal character.

If you follow the instructions on the next page you will soon be able to work out exactly what zodiac sign the Moon occupied on the day that you were born and you can then go on to compare the reading for this position with those of your Sun sign and your Ascendant. It is partly the comparison between these three important positions that goes towards making you the unique individual you are.

HOW TO DISCOVER YOUR MOON SIGN

This is a three-stage process. You may need a pen and a piece of paper but if you follow the instructions below the process should only take a minute or so.

STAGE 1 First of all you need to know the Moon Age at the time of your birth. If you look at Moon Table 1, on page 33, you will find all the years between 1910 and 2008 down the left side. Find the year of your birth and then trace across to the right to the month of your birth. Where the two intersect you will find a number. This is the date of the New Moon in the month that you were born. You now need to count forward the number of days between the New Moon and your own birthday. For example, if the New Moon in the month of your birth was shown as being the 6th and you were born on the 20th, your Moon Age Day would be 14. If the New Moon in the month of your birth came after your birthday, you need to count forward from the New Moon in the previous month. If you were born in a Leap Year, remember to count the 29th February. You can tell if your birth year was a Leap Year if the last two digits can be divided by four. Whatever the result, jot this number down so that you do not forget it.

STAGE 2 Take a look at Moon Table 2 on page 34. Down the left hand column look for the date of your birth. Now trace across to the month of your birth. Where the two meet you will find a letter. Copy this letter down alongside your Moon Age Day.

STAGE 3 Moon Table 3 on page 34 will supply you with the zodiac sign the Moon occupied on the day of your birth. Look for your Moon Age Day down the left hand column and then for the letter you found in Stage 2. Where the two converge you will find a zodiac sign and this is the sign occupied by the Moon on the day that you were born.

Your Zodiac Moon Sign Explained

You will find a profile of all zodiac Moon Signs on pages 35 to 38, showing in yet another way how astrology helps to make you into the individual that you are. In each daily entry of the Astral Diary you can find the zodiac position of the Moon for every day of the year. This also allows you to discover your lunar birthdays. Since the Moon passes through all the signs of the zodiac in about a month, you can expect something like twelve lunar birthdays each year. At these times you are likely to be emotionally steady and able to make the sort of decisions that have real, lasting value.

MOON TABLE 1

YEAR	SEP	OCT	NOV	YEAR	SEP	OCT	NOV	YEAR	SEP	OCT	NOV
1910	3	2	1	1943	29	29	27	1976	23	23	21
1911	22	21	20	1944	17	17	15	1977	13	12	11
1912	12	11	9	1945	6	6	4	1978	2	2/31	30
1913	30	29	28	1946	25	24	23	1979	21	20	19
1914	19	19	17	1947	14	14	12	1980	10	9	8
1915	9	8	7	1948	3	2	1	1981	28	27	26
1916	27	27	26	1949	23	21	20	1982	17	17	15
1917	15	15	14	1950	12	11	9	1983	7	6	4
1918	4	4	3	1951	1	1/30	29	1984	25	24	22
1919	23	23	22	1952	19	18	17	1985	14	14	12
1920	12	12	10	1953	8	8	6	1986	4	3	2
1921	2	1/30	29	1954	27	26	25	1987	23	22	21
1922	21	20	19	1955	16	15	14	1988	11	10	9
1923	10	10	8	1956	4	4	2	1989	29	29	28
1924	28	28	26	1957	23	23	21	1990	19	18	17
1925	18	17	16	1958	13	12	11	1991	8	8	6
1926	7	6	5	1959	3	2/31	30	1992	26	25	24
1927	25	25	24	1960	21	20	19	1993	16	15	14
1928	14	14	12	1961	10	9	8	1994	5	5	3
1929	3	2	1	1962	28	28	27	1995	24	24	22
1930	22	20	19	1963	17	17	15	1996	13	11	10
1931	12	11	9	1964	6	5	4	1997	2	2/31	30
1932	30	29	27	1965	25	24	22	1998	20	20	19
1933	19	19	17	1966	14	14	12	1999	9	9	8
1934	9	8	7	1967	4	3	2	2000	27	27	26
1935	27	27	26	1968	23	22	21	2001	17	17	16
1936	15	15	14	1969	11	10	9	2002	6	6	4
1937	4	4	3	1970	1	1/30	29	2003	26	25	24
1938	23	23	22	1971	19	19	18	2004	13	12	11
1939	13	12	11	1972	8	8	6	2005	3	2	1
1940	2	1/30	29	1973	27	26	25	2006	22	21	20
1941	21	20	19	1974	16	15	14	2007	12	11	9
1942	10	10	8	1975	5	5	3	2008	30	29	28

TABLE 2   MOON TABLE 3

DAY	OCT	NOV	M/D	a	b	d	e	f	g	i
1	a	e	0	LI	LI	LI	SC	SC	SC	SA
2	a	e	1	LI	LI	SC	SC	SC	SA	SA
3	a	e	2	LI	SC	SC	SC	SA	SA	CP
4	b	f	3	SC	SC	SC	SA	SA	CP	CP
5	b	f	4	SC	SA	SA	SA	CP	CP	CP
6	b	f	5	SA	SA	SA	CP	CP	AQ	AQ
7	b	f	6	SA	CP	CP	CP	AQ	AQ	AQ
8	b	f	7	SA	CP	CP	AQ	AQ	PI	PI
9	b	f	8	CP	CP	CP	AQ	PI	PI	PI
10	b	f	9	CP	AQ	AQ	AQ	PI	PI	AR
11	b	f	10	AQ	AQ	AQ	PI	AR	AR	AR
12	b	f	11	AQ	PI	PI	PI	AR	AR	TA
13	b	g	12	PI	PI	PI	AR	TA	TA	TA
14	d	g	13	PI	AR	PI	AR	TA	TA	GE
15	d	g	14	AR	AR	AR	TA	GE	GE	GE
16	d	g	15	AR	AR	AR	TA	TA	TA	GE
17	d	g	16	AR	AR	TA	TA	GE	GE	GE
18	d	g	17	AR	TA	TA	GE	GE	GE	CA
19	d	g	18	TA	TA	GE	GE	GE	CA	CA
20	d	g	19	TA	TA	GE	GE	CA	CA	CA
21	d	g	20	GE	GE	GE	CA	CA	CA	LE
22	d	g	21	GE	GE	CA	CA	CA	LE	LE
23	d	i	22	GE	CA	CA	CA	LE	LE	VI
24	e	i	23	CA	CA	CA	LE	LE	LE	VI
25	e	i	24	CA	CA	LE	LE	LE	VI	VI
26	e	i	25	CA	LE	LE	LE	VI	VI	LI
27	e	i	26	LE	LE	VI	VI	VI	LI	LI
28	e	i	27	LE	VI	VI	VI	LI	LI	SC
29	e	i	28	VI	VI	VI	LI	LI	LI	SC
30	e	i	29	VI	VI	LI	LI	LI	SC	SC
31	e	–								

AR = Aries, TA = Taurus, GE = Gemini, CA = Cancer, LE = Leo, VI = Virgo, LI = Libra, SC = Scorpio, SA = Sagittarius, CP = Capricorn, AQ = Aquarius, PI = Pisces

MOON SIGNS

Moon in Aries

You have a strong imagination, courage, determination and a desire to do things in your own way and forge your own path through life.

Originality is a key attribute; you are seldom stuck for ideas although your mind is changeable and you could take the time to focus on individual tasks. Often quick-tempered, you take orders from few people and live life at a fast pace. Avoid health problems by taking regular time out for rest and relaxation.

Emotionally, it is important that you talk to those you are closest to and work out your true feelings. Once you discover that people are there to help, there is less necessity for you to do everything yourself.

Moon in Taurus

The Moon in Taurus gives you a courteous and friendly manner, which means you are likely to have many friends.

The good things in life mean a lot to you, as Taurus is an Earth sign that delights in experiences which please the senses. Hence you are probably a lover of good food and drink, which may in turn mean you need to keep an eye on the bathroom scales, especially as looking good is also important to you.

Emotionally you are fairly stable and you stick by your own standards. Taureans do not respond well to change. Intuition also plays an important part in your life.

Moon in Gemini

You have a warm-hearted character, sympathetic and eager to help others. At times reserved, you can also be articulate and chatty: this is part of the paradox of Gemini, which always brings duplicity to the nature. You are interested in current affairs, have a good intellect, and are good company and likely to have many friends. Most of your friends have a high opinion of you and would be ready to defend you should the need arise. However, this is usually unnecessary, as you are quite capable of defending yourself in any verbal confrontation.

Travel is important to your inquisitive mind and you find intellectual stimulus in mixing with people from different cultures. You also gain much from reading, writing and the arts but you do need plenty of rest and relaxation in order to avoid fatigue.

Moon in Cancer

The Moon in Cancer at the time of birth is a fortunate position as Cancer is the Moon's natural home. This means that the qualities of compassion and understanding given by the Moon are especially enhanced in your nature, and you are friendly and sociable and cope well with emotional pressures. You cherish home and family life, and happily do the domestic tasks. Your surroundings are important to you and you hate squalor and filth. You are likely to have a love of music and poetry.

Your basic character, although at times changeable like the Moon itself, depends on symmetry. You aim to make your surroundings comfortable and harmonious, for yourself and those close to you.

Moon in Leo

The best qualities of the Moon and Leo come together to make you warm-hearted, fair, ambitious and self-confident. With good organisational abilities, you invariably rise to a position of responsibility in your chosen career. This is fortunate as you don't enjoy being an 'also-ran' and would rather be an important part of a small organisation than a menial in a large one.

You should be lucky in love, and happy, provided you put in the effort to make a comfortable home for yourself and those close to you. It is likely that you will have a love of pleasure, sport, music and literature. Life brings you many rewards, most of them as a direct result of your own efforts, although you may be luckier than average and ready to make the best of any situation.

Moon in Virgo

You are endowed with good mental abilities and a keen receptive memory, but you are never ostentatious or pretentious. Naturally quite reserved, you still have many friends, especially of the opposite sex. Marital relationships must be discussed carefully and worked at so that they remain harmonious, as personal attachments can be a problem if you do not give them your full attention.

Talented and persevering, you possess artistic qualities and are a good homemaker. Earning your honours through genuine merit, you work long and hard towards your objectives but show little pride in your achievements. Many short journeys will be undertaken in your life.

Moon in Libra

With the Moon in Libra you are naturally popular and make friends easily. People like you, probably more than you realise, you bring fun to a party and are a natural diplomat. For all its good points, Libra is not the most stable of astrological signs and, as a result, your emotions can be a little unstable too. Therefore, although the Moon in Libra is said to be good for love and marriage, your Sun sign and Rising sign will have an important effect on your emotional and loving qualities.

You must remember to relate to others in your decision-making. Co-operation is crucial because Libra represents the 'balance' of life that can only be achieved through harmonious relationships. Conformity is not easy for you because Libra, an Air sign, likes its independence.

Moon in Scorpio

Some people might call you pushy. In fact, all you really want to do is to live life to the full and protect yourself and your family from the pressures of life. Take care to avoid giving the impression of being sarcastic or impulsive and use your energies wisely and constructively.

You have great courage and you invariably achieve your goals by force of personality and sheer effort. You are fond of mystery and are good at predicting the outcome of situations and events. Travel experiences can be beneficial to you.

You may experience problems if you do not take time to examine your motives in a relationship, and also if you allow jealousy, always a feature of Scorpio, to cloud your judgement.

Moon in Sagittarius

The Moon in Sagittarius helps to make you a generous individual with humanitarian qualities and a kind heart. Restlessness may be intrinsic as your mind is seldom still. Perhaps because of this, you have a need for change that could lead you to several major moves during your adult life. You are not afraid to stand your ground when you know your judgement is right, you speak directly and have good intuition.

At work you are quick, efficient and versatile and so you make an ideal employee. You need work to be intellectually demanding and do not enjoy tedious routines.

In relationships, you anger quickly if faced with stupidity or deception, though you are just as quick to forgive and forget. Emotionally, there are times when your heart rules your head.

Moon in Capricorn

The Moon in Capricorn makes you popular and likely to come into the public eye in some way. The watery Moon is not entirely comfortable in the Earth sign of Capricorn and this may lead to some difficulties in the early years of life. An initial lack of creative ability and indecision must be overcome before the true qualities of patience and perseverance inherent in Capricorn can show through.

You have good administrative ability and are a capable worker, and if you are careful you can accumulate wealth. But you must be cautious and take professional advice in partnerships, as you are open to deception. You may be interested in social or welfare work, which suit your organisational skills and sympathy for others.

Moon in Aquarius

The Moon in Aquarius makes you an active and agreeable person with a friendly, easy-going nature. Sympathetic to the needs of others, you flourish in a laid-back atmosphere. You are broad-minded, fair and open to suggestion, although sometimes you have an unconventional quality which others can find hard to understand.

You are interested in the strange and curious, and in old articles and places. You enjoy trips to these places and gain much from them. Political, scientific and educational work interests you and you might choose a career in science or technology.

Money-wise, you make gains through innovation and concentration and Lunar Aquarians often tackle more than one job at a time. In love you are kind and honest.

Moon in Pisces

You have a kind, sympathetic nature, somewhat retiring at times, but you always take account of others' feelings and help when you can.

Personal relationships may be problematic, but as life goes on you can learn from your experiences and develop a better understanding of yourself and the world around you.

You have a fondness for travel, appreciate beauty and harmony and hate disorder and strife. You may be fond of literature and would make a good writer or speaker yourself. You have a creative imagination and may come across as an incurable romantic. You have strong intuition, maybe bordering on a mediumistic quality, which sets you apart from the mass. You may not be rich in cash terms, but your personal gifts are worth more than gold.

SCORPIO IN LOVE

Discover how compatible you are with people from the same and other parts of the zodiac. Five stars equals a match made in heaven!

Scorpio meets Scorpio

Scorpio is deep, complex and enigmatic, traits which often lead to misunderstanding with other zodiac signs, so a double Scorpio match can work well because both parties understand one another. They will allow each other periods of silence and reflection but still be willing to help, advise and support when necessary. Their relationship may seem odd to others but that doesn't matter if those involved are happy. All in all, an unusual but contented combination. Star rating: *****

Scorpio meets Sagittarius

Sagittarius needs constant stimulation and loves to be busy from dawn till dusk which may mean that it feels rather frustrated by Scorpio. Scorpions are hard workers, too, but they are also contemplative and need periods of quiet which may mean that they appear dull to Sagittarius. This could lead to a gulf between the two which must be overcome. With time and patience on both sides, this can be a lucrative encounter and good in terms of home and family. A variable alliance. Star rating: ***

Scorpio meets Capricorn

Lack of communication is the governing factor here. Neither of this pair are renowned communicators and both need a partner to draw out their full verbal potential. Consequently, Scorpio may find Capricorn cold and unapproachable while Capricorn could find Scorpio dark and brooding. Both are naturally tidy and would keep a pristine house but great effort and a mutual goal is needed on both sides to overcome the missing spark. A good match on the financial side, but probably not an earthshattering personal encounter. Star rating: **

Scorpio meets Aquarius

This is a promising and practical combination. Scorpio responds well to Aquarius' exploration of its deep nature and so this shy sign becomes lighter, brighter and more inspirational. Meanwhile, Aquarians are rarely as sure of themselves as they like to appear and are reassured by Scorpio's steady and determined support. Both signs want to be kind to the other which is a basis for a relationship that should be warm most of the time and extremely hot occasionally. Star rating: ****

Scorpio meets Pisces

If ever there were two zodiac signs that have a total rapport, it has to be Scorpio and Pisces. They share very similar needs: they are not gregarious and are happy with a little silence, good music and time to contemplate the finer things in life, and both are attracted to family life. Apart, they can have a tendency to wander in a romantic sense, but this is reduced when they come together. They are deep, firm friends who enjoy each other's company and this must lead to an excellent chance of success. These people are surely made for each other! Star rating: *****

Scorpio meets Aries

There can be great affection here, even if the two signs are so very different. The common link is the planet Mars, which plays a part in both these natures. Although Aries is, outwardly, the most dominant, Scorpio people are among the most powerful to be found anywhere. This quiet determination is respected by Aries. Aries will satisfy the passionate side of Scorpio, particularly with instruction from Scorpio. There are mysteries here which will add spice to life. The few arguments that do occur are likely to be awe-inspiring. Star rating: ****

Scorpio meets Taurus

Scorpio is deep – very deep – which may be a problem, because Taurus doesn't wear its heart on its sleeve either. It might be difficult for this pair to get together, because neither is naturally inclined to make the first move. Taurus stands in awe of the power and intensity of the Scorpio mind, while the Scorpion is interested in the Bull's affable and friendly qualities, so an enduring relationship could be forged if the couple ever get round to talking. Both are lovers of home and family, which will help to cement a relationship. Star rating: **

Scorpio meets Gemini

There could be problems here. Scorpio is one of the deepest and least understood of all the zodiac signs, which at first seems like a challenge to intellectual Gemini, who thinks it can solve anything. But the deeper the Gemini digs, the further down Scorpio goes. Meanwhile, Scorpio may be finding Gemini thoughtless, shallow and even downright annoying. Gemini is often afraid of Scorpio's perception and strength, together with the sting in the Scorpion's tail. Anything is possible, but the outlook for this match is less than promising. Star rating: **

Scorpio meets Cancer

This match is potentially a great success, a fact which is often a mystery to astrologers. Some feel it is due to the compatibility of the Water element, but it could also come from a mixture of similarity and difference in the personalities. Scorpio is partly ruled by Mars, which gives it a deep, passionate, dominant and powerful side. Cancerians generally like and respect this amalgam, and recognise something there that they would like to adopt themselves. On the other side of the coin, Scorpio needs love and emotional security which Cancer offers generously. Star rating: *****

Scorpio meets Leo

Stand back and watch the sparks fly! Scorpio has the deep sensitivity of a Water sign but it is also partially ruled by Fire planet Mars, from which it draws great power, and Leo will find that difficult. Leo loves to take charge and really hates to feel psychologically undermined, which is Scorpio's stock-in-trade. Scorpio may find Leo's ideals a little shallow, which will be upsetting to the Lion. Anything is possible, but this possibility is rather slimmer than most. Star rating: **

Scorpio meets Virgo

There are one or two potential difficulties here, but there is also a meeting point from which to overcome them. Virgo is very caring and protective, a trait which Scorpio understands and even emulates. Scorpio will impress Virgo with its serious side. Both signs are consistent, although also sarcastic. Scorpio may uncover a hidden passion in Virgo which all too often lies deep within its Earth-sign nature. Material success is very likely, with Virgo taking the lion's share of the domestic chores and family responsibilities. Star rating: ***

Scorpio meets Libra

Many astrologers have reservations about this match because, on the surface, the signs are so different. However, this couple may find fulfilment because these differences mean that their respective needs are met. Scorpio needs a partner to lighten the load, which won't daunt Libra, while Libra looks for a steadfast quality which it doesn't possess, but which Scorpio can supply naturally. Financial success is possible because they both have good ideas and back them up with hard work and determination. All in all, a promising outlook. Star rating: ****

VENUS:
THE PLANET OF LOVE

If you look up at the sky around sunset or sunrise you will often see Venus in close attendance to the Sun. It is arguably one of the most beautiful sights of all and there is little wonder that historically it became associated with the goddess of love. But although Venus does play an important part in the way you view love and in the way others see you romantically, this is only one of the spheres of influence that it enjoys in your overall character.

Venus has a part to play in the more cultured side of your life and has much to do with your appreciation of art, literature, music and general creativity. Even the way you look is responsive to the part of the zodiac that Venus occupied at the start of your life, though this fact is also down to your Sun sign and Ascending sign. If, at the time you were born, Venus occupied one of the more gregarious zodiac signs, you will be more likely to wear your heart on your sleeve, as well as to be more attracted to entertainment, social gatherings and good company. If on the other hand Venus occupied a quiet zodiac sign at the time of your birth, you would tend to be more retiring and less willing to shine in public situations.

It's good to know what part the planet Venus plays in your life for it can have a great bearing on the way you appear to the rest of the world and since we all have to mix with others, you can learn to make the very best of what Venus has to offer you.

One of the great complications in the past has always been trying to establish exactly what zodiac position Venus enjoyed when you were born because the planet is notoriously difficult to track. However, we have solved that problem by creating a table that is exclusive to your Sun sign, which you will find on the following page.

Establishing your Venus sign could not be easier. Just look up the year of your birth on the next page and you will see a sign of the zodiac. This was the sign that Venus occupied in the period covered by your sign in that year. If Venus occupied more than one sign during the period, this is indicated by the date on which the sign changed, and the name of the new sign. For instance, if you were born in 1950, Venus was in Libra until the 28th October, after which time it was in Scorpio. If you were born before 28th October your Venus sign is Libra, if you were born on or after 28th October, your Venus sign is Scorpio. Once you have established the position of Venus at the time of your birth, you can then look in the pages which follow to see how this has a bearing on your life as a whole.

1910 LIBRA / 30.10 SCORPIO
1911 VIRGO / 9.11 LIBRA
1912 SCORPIO / 24.10 SAGITTARIUS /
    18.11 CAPRICORN
1913 LIBRA / 14.11 SCORPIO
1914 SAGITTARIUS / 16.11 SCORPIO
1915 SCORPIO / 9.11 SAGITTARIUS
1916 VIRGO / 3.11 LIBRA
1917 SAGITTARIUS / 7.11 CAPRICORN
1918 LIBRA / 30.10 SCORPIO
1919 VIRGO / 9.11 LIBRA
1920 SCORPIO / 24.10 SAGITTARIUS /
    17.11 CAPRICORN
1921 LIBRA / 14.11 SCORPIO
1922 SAGITTARIUS / 16.11 SCORPIO
1923 SCORPIO / 9.11 SAGITTARIUS
1924 VIRGO / 3.11 LIBRA
1925 SAGITTARIUS / 7.11 CAPRICORN
1926 LIBRA / 29.10 SCORPIO
1927 VIRGO / 10.11 LIBRA
1928 SAGITTARIUS /
    17.11 CAPRICORN
1929 LIBRA / 13.11 SCORPIO
1930 SAGITTARIUS / 16.11 SCORPIO
1931 SCORPIO / 8.11 SAGITTARIUS
1932 VIRGO / 2.11 LIBRA
1933 SAGITTARIUS / 7.11 CAPRICORN
1934 LIBRA / 29.10 SCORPIO
1935 VIRGO / 10.11 LIBRA
1936 SAGITTARIUS / 16.11 CAPRICORN
1937 LIBRA / 13.11 SCORPIO
1938 SAGITTARIUS / 16.11 SCORPIO
1939 SCORPIO / 7.11 SAGITTARIUS
1940 VIRGO / 2.11 LIBRA
1941 SAGITTARIUS / 7.11 CAPRICORN
1942 LIBRA / 28.10 SCORPIO
1943 VIRGO / 10.11 LIBRA
1944 SAGITTARIUS / 16.11 CAPRICORN
1945 LIBRA / 13.11 SCORPIO
1946 SAGITTARIUS / 16.11 SCORPIO
1947 SCORPIO / 6.11 SAGITTARIUS
1948 VIRGO / 1.11 LIBRA
1949 SAGITTARIUS / 6.11 CAPRICORN
1950 LIBRA / 28.10 SCORPIO
1951 VIRGO / 10.11 LIBRA
1952 SAGITTARIUS / 16.11 CAPRICORN
1953 LIBRA / 12.11 SCORPIO
1954 SAGITTARIUS / 28.10 SCORPIO
1955 SCORPIO / 6.11 SAGITTARIUS
1956 VIRGO / 1.11 LIBRA
1957 SAGITTARIUS / 6.11 CAPRICORN
1958 LIBRA / 27.10 SCORPIO
1959 VIRGO / 10.11 LIBRA
1960 SAGITTARIUS /
    15.11 CAPRICORN

1961 LIBRA / 12.11 SCORPIO
1962 SAGITTARIUS / 28.10 SCORPIO
1963 SCORPIO / 5.11 SAGITTARIUS
1964 VIRGO / 31.10 LIBRA
1965 SAGITTARIUS / 6.11 CAPRICORN
1966 LIBRA / 27.10 SCORPIO
1967 VIRGO / 10.11 LIBRA
1968 SAGITTARIUS /
    15.11 CAPRICORN
1969 LIBRA / 11.11 SCORPIO
1970 SAGITTARIUS / 28.10 SCORPIO
1971 SCORPIO / 4.11 SAGITTARIUS
1972 VIRGO / 31.10 LIBRA
1973 SAGITTARIUS / 6.11 CAPRICORN
1974 LIBRA / 26.10 SCORPIO
1975 VIRGO / 9.11 LIBRA
1976 SAGITTARIUS /
    15.11 CAPRICORN
1977 LIBRA / 11.11 SCORPIO
1978 SAGITTARIUS / 28.10 SCORPIO
1979 SCORPIO / 4.11 SAGITTARIUS
1980 VIRGO / 30.10 LIBRA
1981 SAGITTARIUS / 5.11 CAPRICORN
1982 LIBRA / 26.10 SCORPIO
1983 VIRGO / 9.11 LIBRA
1984 SAGITTARIUS /
    14.11 CAPRICORN
1985 LIBRA / 10.11 SCORPIO
1986 SAGITTARIUS / 28.10 SCORPIO
1987 SCORPIO / 3.11 SAGITTARIUS
1988 VIRGO / 30.10 LIBRA
1989 SAGITTARIUS / 5.11 CAPRICORN
1990 LIBRA / 25.10 SCORPIO
1991 VIRGO / 9.11 LIBRA
1992 SAGITTARIUS /
    14.11 CAPRICORN
1993 LIBRA / 10.11 SCORPIO
1994 SAGITTARIUS / 28.10 SCORPIO
1995 SCORPIO / 3.11 SAGITTARIUS
1996 VIRGO / 29.10 LIBRA
1997 SAGITTARIUS / 5.11 CAPRICORN
1998 LIBRA / 25.10 SCORPIO
1999 VIRGO / 9.11 LIBRA
2000 SAGITTARIUS /
    14.11 CAPRICORN
2001 LIBRA / 10.11 SCORPIO
2002 SAGITTARIUS / 28.10 SCORPIO
2003 SCORPIO / 3.11 SAGITTARIUS
2004 VIRGO / 29.10 LIBRA
2005 SAGITTARIUS / 5.11 CAPRICORN
2006 LIBRA / 25.10 SCORPIO
2007 VIRGO / 9.11 LIBRA
2008 SAGITTARIUS / 14.11 CAPRICORN

44

VENUS THROUGH THE ZODIAC SIGNS

Venus in Aries

Amongst other things, the position of Venus in Aries indicates a fondness for travel, music and all creative pursuits. Your nature tends to be affectionate and you would try not to create confusion or difficulty for others if it could be avoided. Many people with this planetary position have a great love of the theatre, and mental stimulation is of the greatest importance. Early romantic attachments are common with Venus in Aries, so it is very important to establish a genuine sense of romantic continuity. Early marriage is not recommended, especially if it is based on sympathy. You may give your heart a little too readily on occasions.

Venus in Taurus

You are capable of very deep feelings and your emotions tend to last for a very long time. This makes you a trusting partner and lover, whose constancy is second to none. In life you are precise and careful and always try to do things the right way. Although this means an ordered life, which you are comfortable with, it can also lead you to be rather too fussy for your own good. Despite your pleasant nature, you are very fixed in your opinions and quite able to speak your mind. Others are attracted to you and historical astrologers always quoted this position of Venus as being very fortunate in terms of marriage. However, if you find yourself involved in a failed relationship, it could take you a long time to trust again.

Venus in Gemini

As with all associations related to Gemini, you tend to be quite versatile, anxious for change and intelligent in your dealings with the world at large. You may gain money from more than one source but you are equally good at spending it. There is an inference here that you are a good communicator, via either the written or the spoken word, and you love to be in the company of interesting people. Always on the look-out for culture, you may also be very fond of music, and love to indulge the curious and cultured side of your nature. In romance you tend to have more than one relationship and could find yourself associated with someone who has previously been a friend or even a distant relative.

Venus in Cancer

You often stay close to home because you are very fond of family and enjoy many of your most treasured moments when you are with those you love. Being naturally sympathetic, you will always do anything you can to support those around you, even people you hardly know at all. This charitable side of your nature is your most noticeable trait and is one of the reasons why others are naturally so fond of you. Being receptive and in some cases even psychic, you can see through to the soul of most of those with whom you come into contact. You may not commence too many romantic attachments but when you do give your heart, it tends to be unconditionally.

Venus in Leo

It must become quickly obvious to almost anyone you meet that you are kind, sympathetic and yet determined enough to stand up for anyone or anything that is truly important to you. Bright and sunny, you warm the world with your natural enthusiasm and would rarely do anything to hurt those around you, or at least not intentionally. In romance you are ardent and sincere, though some may find your style just a little overpowering. Gains come through your contacts with other people and this could be especially true with regard to romance, for love and money often come hand in hand for those who were born with Venus in Leo. People claim to understand you, though you are more complex than you seem.

Venus in Virgo

Your nature could well be fairly quiet no matter what your Sun sign might be, though this fact often manifests itself as an inner peace and would not prevent you from being basically sociable. Some delays and even the odd disappointment in love cannot be ruled out with this planetary position, though it's a fact that you will usually find the happiness you look for in the end. Catapulting yourself into romantic entanglements that you know to be rather ill-advised is not sensible, and it would be better to wait before you committed yourself exclusively to any one person. It is the essence of your nature to serve the world at large and through doing so it is possible that you will attract money at some stage in your life.

Venus in Libra

Venus is very comfortable in Libra and bestows upon those people who have this planetary position a particular sort of kindness that is easy to recognise. This is a very good position for all sorts of friendships and also for romantic attachments that usually bring much joy into your life. Few individuals with Venus in Libra would avoid marriage and since you are capable of great depths of love, it is likely that you will find a contented personal life. You like to mix with people of integrity and intelligence but don't take kindly to scruffy surroundings or work that means getting your hands too dirty. Careful speculation, good business dealings and money through marriage all seem fairly likely.

Venus in Scorpio

You are quite open and tend to spend money quite freely, even on those occasions when you don't have very much. Although your intentions are always good, there are times when you get yourself in to the odd scrape and this can be particularly true when it comes to romance, which you may come to late or from a rather unexpected direction. Certainly you have the power to be happy and to make others contented on the way, but you find the odd stumbling block on your journey through life and it could seem that you have to work harder than those around you. As a result of this, you gain a much deeper understanding of the true value of personal happiness than many people ever do, and are likely to achieve true contentment in the end.

Venus in Sagittarius

You are lighthearted, cheerful and always able to see the funny side of any situation. These facts enhance your popularity, which is especially high with members of the opposite sex. You should never have to look too far to find romantic interest in your life, though it is just possible that you might be too willing to commit yourself before you are certain that the person in question is right for you. Part of the problem here extends to other areas of life too. The fact is that you like variety in everything and so can tire of situations that fail to offer it. All the same, if you choose wisely and learn to understand your restless side, then great happiness can be yours.

Venus in Capricorn

The most notable trait that comes from Venus in this position is that it makes you trustworthy and able to take on all sorts of responsibilities in life. People are instinctively fond of you and love you all the more because you are always ready to help those who are in any form of need. Social and business popularity can be yours and there is a magnetic quality to your nature that is particularly attractive in a romantic sense. Anyone who wants a partner for a lover, a spouse and a good friend too would almost certainly look in your direction. Constancy is the hallmark of your nature and unfaithfulness would go right against the grain. You might sometimes be a little too trusting.

Venus in Aquarius

This location of Venus offers a fondness for travel and a desire to try out something new at every possible opportunity. You are extremely easy to get along with and tend to have many friends from varied backgrounds, classes and inclinations. You like to live a distinct sort of life and gain a great deal from moving about, both in a career sense and with regard to your home. It is not out of the question that you could form a romantic attachment to someone who comes from far away or be attracted to a person of a distinctly artistic and original nature. What you cannot stand is jealousy, for you have friends of both sexes and would want to keep things that way.

Venus in Pisces

The first thing people tend to notice about you is your wonderful, warm smile. Being very charitable by nature you will do anything to help others, even if you don't know them well. Much of your life may be spent sorting out situations for other people, but it is very important to feel that you are living for yourself too. In the main, you remain cheerful, and tend to be quite attractive to members of the opposite sex. Where romantic attachments are concerned, you could be drawn to people who are significantly older or younger than yourself or to someone with a unique career or point of view. It might be best for you to avoid marrying whilst you are still very young.

SCORPIO:
2007 DIARY PAGES

October
2007

1 MONDAY
Moon Age Day 19   Moon Sign Gemini

Today offers you scope to experience life at an emotional level. Intuition is strong and can guide you accurately when it comes to making the right decisions, though you may not be as practical as would often be the case. As the day wears on your more vocal side is to the fore, especially when you're with friends.

2 TUESDAY
Moon Age Day 20   Moon Sign Gemini

Your selfless attitude has a strong part to play in relationships at this time. Be prepared to show your willingness to do almost anything for others, especially in terms of family relationships. If you are not getting on at work quite as well as you would wish, your best response is to show a little patience.

3 WEDNESDAY
Moon Age Day 21   Moon Sign Cancer

It's possible that what once seemed like a sound and practical idea is now less appealing, and you could find that you are working very hard to no real end. One fact about Scorpio that is always present is your resistance to giving in, and though this is usually a laudable quality, it might mean even more toil for nothing now.

4 THURSDAY
Moon Age Day 22   Moon Sign Cancer

This would be an excellent time to travel for fun. Even if what you are doing is entirely practical in nature, you can enjoy yourself on the way. There has rarely been a better time for Scorpio to mix business with pleasure, and you can seek out chances to revel in the company of the sort of people who have a delightful madness about them.

5 FRIDAY
Moon Age Day 23   Moon Sign Leo

Information you can get from colleagues and friends now might help you to throw some light on a mystery from the past. Try to reach out to people in different walks of life and learn from what they have to say. You are gradually climbing into a much stronger personal position and should be getting back some of that earlier optimism.

6 SATURDAY
Moon Age Day 24   Moon Sign Leo

Finances and material concerns are not highlighted to the same extent as they were a few days ago. The weekend is more about enjoying yourself rather than increasing your income. Your greatest source of reward comes from being able to get yourself in the right sort of company and from opening up more.

7 SUNDAY
Moon Age Day 25   Moon Sign Leo

This would be a good day to do something recreational. At the same time you can be quite creative and can use this trait to produce results from all your efforts. On a slightly negative slant you need to be careful about what you say in open discussions. It is quite possible to give offence without intending to do so.

8 MONDAY
Moon Age Day 26   Moon Sign Virgo

You can now capitalise on a phase of busy action. Mercury has entered your solar first house and this enables you to pep up your life no end. Communications generally are well starred, and there is a certain sense of excitement that is going to be around for a week or two at least. You certainly should not get bored.

9 TUESDAY
Moon Age Day 27   Moon Sign Virgo

If you need some help today, it shouldn't be very far away. You should also find moments for quiet reflection, which is necessary if the actions you are going to take are well thought out. It's worth allowing family members a little more leeway than might have been the case recently.

10 WEDNESDAY   *Moon Age Day 28   Moon Sign Libra*

As the Moon is now in your solar twelfth house, you could be a bit more socially reluctant than usual. Trends encourage an urge to spend moments on your own, and you may decide not to get involved in anything new for the next couple of days. None of this should prevent you from being well organised or professionally active.

11 THURSDAY   *Moon Age Day 0   Moon Sign Libra*

You natural sense of compassion now assists you to help those who are less well off than you are. This is also a good time to be with friends, but not a particularly useful period for inviting strangers into your life. You may still not be firing on all cylinders in a strictly social sense.

12 FRIDAY   ☿   *Moon Age Day 1   Moon Sign Libra*

With a slow start to the day you might be very surprised at the way things speed up later on. Your best approach under current influences is to avoid pointless routines and spend as much time as you can thinking about the new possibilities that stand all around you. By tomorrow you should be in a position to get stuck in big time.

13 SATURDAY   ☿   *Moon Age Day 2   Moon Sign Scorpio*

The Moon now moves into Scorpio. This fact, taken together with that first-house Mercury, helps you to make this the most dynamic day of the month. If you can get Lady Luck on your side, you can afford to take more risks in the knowledge that your capacity for looking and thinking ahead is extremely good.

14 SUNDAY   ☿   *Moon Age Day 3   Moon Sign Scorpio*

If you have a pet project, now is the best time of all to work on it. You can persuade almost everyone to lend a hand and if there is any problem at all about today it lies in the fact that your very popularity makes it difficult to concentrate. You would be wise to stay away from arguments that have nothing to do with you.

15 MONDAY ☿ *Moon Age Day 4   Moon Sign Sagittarius*

Money-making concerns are highlighted, and you can use your knack of hanging on to cash you already possess. Don't be surprised if you discover that you have an admirer you didn't suspect previously. In every sense you can make sure your popularity is going off the scale.

16 TUESDAY ☿ *Moon Age Day 5   Moon Sign Sagittarius*

Communication is positively highlighted under present trends, and you are also in a good position to see all sides of specific issues. In a work sense you should not provide opponents with the very ammunition they need by admitted your shortcomings. The truth is important, but only up to a point today.

17 WEDNESDAY ☿ *Moon Age Day 6   Moon Sign Sagittarius*

You may meet someone today who challenges your views or who really makes you work hard to explain yourself. This is not necessarily a bad thing, especially if it shakes you out of some sort of lethargy that has overtaken you. You needn't let anything threaten your overall success.

18 THURSDAY ☿ *Moon Age Day 7   Moon Sign Capricorn*

There are signs that you may spend a lot of time at the moment trying to work out what loved ones are thinking. This is not a wasted exercise because as a result of your efforts you might be able to make someone else much happier. Your concern for those you love is always on display, even when you are busy with other things.

19 FRIDAY ☿ *Moon Age Day 8   Moon Sign Capricorn*

Your desire for knowledge is to the fore, encouraging you to spend a lot of time today casting around to make yourself even more knowledgeable. Not only do you want to know things but you also want to communicate what you have learned to others. There are gains to be made financially, but not by gambling.

20 SATURDAY ☿ *Moon Age Day 9   Moon Sign Aquarius*

This is a day to gain some domestic tranquillity and a period during which you may be happy to spend time in the bosom of your family. You can push yourself to other things if you really try, though it could seem that small blockages are placed upon your actions. Don't worry, because this is an entirely temporary phenomenon.

21 SUNDAY ☿ *Moon Age Day 10   Moon Sign Aquarius*

If ever there was a good time to start new projects, that is what this Sunday represents. You should have the time to think things through and to plan, but not for long if you have a burning desire to get on and achieve something. Neither need your efforts be restricted to domestic or home-based issues.

22 MONDAY ☿ *Moon Age Day 11   Moon Sign Pisces*

You have scope to become the centre of attention as a new working week gets started, and the social aspects of life could now seem just as important as the practical or professional ones. Stand by to go out and discover love, especially if you are presently without a permanent romantic attachment.

23 TUESDAY ☿ *Moon Age Day 12   Moon Sign Pisces*

Your present fondness for debate may now be put to the test, and winning may take some hard work. Not that this fact should trouble you because this is a period during which you are encouraged to sharpen your intellect and to get to grips with issues that have been murky in the past.

24 WEDNESDAY ☿ *Moon Age Day 13   Moon Sign Pisces*

At last the Sun enters your solar first house and the time for personal rejuvenation is at hand. Even if there have been significant obstacles around with the Sun in your twelfth house, you can put all of that out of the way now. The time is right to look towards your objectives with renewed enthusiasm and a greater sense of purpose.

25 THURSDAY ☿ Moon Age Day 14 Moon Sign Aries

Even if your drive to achieve things is getting stronger all the time, a little caution is advised for the moment. You can be too impetuous for your own good, and might be inclined to fly off the handle if things don't go the way you want them to. Why not exercise a little patience and count to ten before reacting?

26 FRIDAY ☿ Moon Age Day 15 Moon Sign Aries

Beware of making any hasty decisions, especially later on today. The lunar low is in the offing and proves to be stronger as it arrives than it will be across the weekend. This may be because Saturday and Sunday bring more personal associations, whereas today could see you in the thick of professional matters.

27 SATURDAY ☿ Moon Age Day 16 Moon Sign Taurus

Although this might not be the most exciting or dynamic day of the month, you needn't let the lunar low spoil what can be a very enjoyable weekend. A day to keep your wishes moderate and your actions considered. If you decide to spend time with family members and friends, you can pack much enjoyment into today.

28 SUNDAY ☿ Moon Age Day 17 Moon Sign Taurus

Trends encourage you to be preoccupied with the past and inclined to give in to nostalgia. The only piece of advice that counts today is to keep yourself entirely focused on the future and to avoid dwelling on matters that have gone. You can afford to help any friends who need your assistance now.

29 MONDAY ☿ *Moon Age Day 18* *Moon Sign Gemini*

Enthusiasm is to the fore and you should be well able to accept the positive trends brought about by the position of the Sun in your solar first house. Most of all you are very creative and can make things happen with just a click of the finger and thumb. Scorpio is a real wizard, and can make everyone take notice.

30 TUESDAY ☿ *Moon Age Day 19* *Moon Sign Gemini*

If you don't express yourself quite as clearly today as seems to be necessary, some misunderstandings can crop up. Do your best to explain yourself fully and especially so if you are dealing with ideas that are quite clear to you but fairly obscure to colleagues and superiors.

31 WEDNESDAY ☿ *Moon Age Day 20* *Moon Sign Cancer*

Freedom is the key to happiness on the last day of October, and you may not be very pleased if circumstances conspire to hold you back in any way. There is a certain restlessness about you today that can best be dealt with by pushing forward and by refusing to take no for an answer.

November

2007

1 THURSDAY ☿ *Moon Age Day 21   Moon Sign Cancer*

There is a strong desire to lead the field as a new month gets started. If you feel that some of your desires are not being met, now is the time to put in the extra effort necessary to bring them to fruition. All of this might make you rather cranky on occasions, especially if circumstances or people get in your way.

2 FRIDAY ☿ *Moon Age Day 22   Moon Sign Leo*

In a social sense you have what it takes to be charming and friendly – just right to improve your general popularity and to get others to help you out. You should be very much at home when in large groups of people and will be quite happy to communicate your ideas to anyone. In almost every sense you can make this a red-letter day.

3 SATURDAY *Moon Age Day 23   Moon Sign Leo*

When it comes to practical matters you can afford to be at the head of things and to take the lead under almost all opportunities. You should remain independent, confident and sure of your point of view. There might be just a little frustration around if other people get in your way or fail to appreciate your point of view.

4 SUNDAY *Moon Age Day 24   Moon Sign Virgo*

Trends assist you to enjoy the cut and thrust of everyday life and to make this Sunday special with just a little extra effort. Rather than concentrating too much on practical matters, it's worth getting out of bed intending to enjoy what comes your way. If an offer of some sort of outing comes along, be prepared to grab it with both hands!

5 MONDAY
Moon Age Day 25   Moon Sign Virgo

Don't be afraid to lap up attention today and take great delight in being the centre of attention. This is likely to be especially true at work, where your motivational skills are also well starred. In a more personal sense you may fail to persuade your partner that you really do know what you are talking about.

6 TUESDAY
Moon Age Day 26   Moon Sign Libra

There are some small gains to be made at the moment, though this is hardly likely to be a sensational sort of day. It's worth planning now for the end of the week because that is when trends come best for you. You shouldn't have any trouble following complicated instructions if you make sure you have your thinking head on.

7 WEDNESDAY
Moon Age Day 27   Moon Sign Libra

You might quite rightly have doubts about those who are talking big but actually producing very little. Your strength, on the other hand, lies in not making promises you cannot follow up on, and in being extremely reliable. Today offers a chance to get in touch with those you know have the answers you presently need.

8 THURSDAY
Moon Age Day 28   Moon Sign Libra

Your sensitivity may affect a loved one in a subtle and quite unexpected way and it is possible that your intuition is also working very strongly. Time spent on your own today is certainly not wasted, and you may even be able to come up with some of the answers that those around you have searched for diligently.

9 FRIDAY
Moon Age Day 0   Moon Sign Scorpio

The lunar high comes as an empowering influence this time round and allows you to make progress in most spheres of your life. You needn't take no for an answer, and tend to be very single-minded when it matters the most. You can also make the most of the fact that your level of general good luck is excellent.

10 SATURDAY *Moon Age Day 1   Moon Sign Scorpio*

You can get the tide of fortune to flow your way, so much so that you are far more willing to take a chance than will have been the case earlier in the week. They say that fortune favours the bold, and if this is the case you are likely to get on very well today. Be brave enough to tell someone how special they are to you.

11 SUNDAY *Moon Age Day 2   Moon Sign Sagittarius*

The ability to deal with practical matters in the way you did yesterday now seems to be slightly lacking. This may be as much down to the reaction of others as it is to your own nature. If there is something about which you are uncertain, you could do far worse than asking someone more experienced.

12 MONDAY *Moon Age Day 3   Moon Sign Sagittarius*

Confidence should be stronger today, and you really notice the first-house Sun that is so strong in your chart at the moment. Make the most of this powerful interlude by committing yourself to plans that are audacious but certainly not impossible. You can make people marvel at your present ability to get things right first time.

13 TUESDAY *Moon Age Day 4   Moon Sign Sagittarius*

Today you can show yourself to be very resourceful and more than able to get what you want, even from potentially difficult situations. You needn't take no for an answer, and can be more persuasive than even Scorpio usually manages to be. Pointless rules and regulations might simply make you more determined.

14 WEDNESDAY *Moon Age Day 5   Moon Sign Capricorn*

You are very inclined to take up mental pursuits today, whether or not they are of practical use to you. Any intellectual challenge could really capture your attention under present trends, so much so that everything else may be ignored. Once again there are gains to made if you show yourself to be single-minded.

15 THURSDAY   *Moon Age Day 6   Moon Sign Capricorn*

Do others presently have your best interests at heart? It might appear so, but you need to be slightly careful because it is entirely possible that at least one person is trying to deceive you in some way. It would be sensible to check and double-check all details today, and to analyse situations very carefully.

16 FRIDAY   *Moon Age Day 7   Moon Sign Aquarius*

Planetary trends now favour hearth and home, and you may not be quite so showy or up-front as has been the case throughout much of this week. Many Scorpios might decide to put their feet up when the day's work is done, and there is certainly nothing wrong with wanting to take a complete break.

17 SATURDAY   *Moon Age Day 8   Moon Sign Aquarius*

Mars is presently in your solar ninth house, and although its position there can help to quicken your mind and also offers flashes of brilliance, there is a downside. It also enhances your argumentative side, especially when others won't go along with something about which you are more than certain.

18 SUNDAY   *Moon Age Day 9   Moon Sign Aquarius*

You have what it takes to be both magnetic and dynamic today, and as a result you can make sure that others love to be around you. The time is right to put your creative powers to the test and start something new around your home. If your ideas are particularly grandiose, you may decide to enlist the support of other family members.

19 MONDAY   *Moon Age Day 10   Moon Sign Pisces*

You now have the ability to go well beyond the status quo and that means really allowing your originality to shine out. The only slight drawback is that you can be a little shy if you have to stand up in front of a crowd. This should be less of a problem whilst the Sun retains its present position.

20 TUESDAY
Moon Age Day 11   Moon Sign Pisces

There are signs that an issue to do with your love life may seem slightly less than inspiring today. Maybe your partner is simply not receptive to your ideas or it could be that they are simply out of sorts with themselves. Whatever the problem, you should be able to find the patience and the sensitivity to deal with it.

21 WEDNESDAY
Moon Age Day 12   Moon Sign Aries

Travel and cultural pursuits are at the top of the agenda now, so some of you may be taking a late but welcome break. This would do you a great deal of good and get you into the right frame of mind to face the upcoming lunar low. Your sense of fun is highlighted and you have what it takes to enjoy good company.

22 THURSDAY
Moon Age Day 13   Moon Sign Aries

This is not what could be called a good period for taking undue risks. Before the end of the day the Moon will have entered Taurus, its worst position as far as you are concerned. Be prepared to use a little circumspection, and don't be afraid to seek out some inspiration and experience when it matters the most.

23 FRIDAY
Moon Age Day 14   Moon Sign Taurus

Your strengths in general are probably not up to par, and you may decide you would rather sit and watch the world go by than be directly involved in almost anything now. That's fine, just as long as you realise that something you have been working hard to achieve needs just a little attention.

24 SATURDAY
Moon Age Day 15   Moon Sign Taurus

Monetary security is to the fore today, and you may decide to sit on your purse or wallet rather than hand over cash when you don't have to do so. When dealing with younger family members you show that you are capable of being strict but fair, though you would also be wise to explain yourself.

61

25 SUNDAY   *Moon Age Day 16   Moon Sign Gemini*

Trends encourage you to bring your experience into play and show yourself to be particularly attentive to the needs of family members. This is a very mixed sort of day but is a period during which you can finalise details for plans that have a bearing on Christmas. Scorpio should definitely be looking ahead now.

26 MONDAY   *Moon Age Day 17   Moon Sign Gemini*

Everyday affairs should run smoothly enough, whilst you have scope to show just how funny you can be. Humour is the way to get what you want at the moment and the fact is hardly likely to be lost on you. All cultural interests captivate you now, and you can make sure your intellect is as honed as a razor under nearly all circumstances.

27 TUESDAY   *Moon Age Day 18   Moon Sign Cancer*

Money and the good things of life generally could be there for the taking, even if you don't recognise the fact at first. Don't be slow when it comes to telling the world what you want, because it's likely that others will be on the same wavelength. You won't achieve anything at all by keeping quiet.

28 WEDNESDAY   *Moon Age Day 19   Moon Sign Cancer*

You may desire greater freedom, but the big question is how to get it? Instead of showing your independence, why not rely on the good offices and ideas of others? At work you can afford to take on responsibility and be speedy in getting things done. Meanwhile, domestic matters are likely to be put on hold.

29 THURSDAY   *Moon Age Day 20   Moon Sign Leo*

When in pursuit of personal achievement you need to be quite subtle today. There is no point in trying to bulldoze others into your way of thinking because you might simply cause them to become more entrenched in their own attitudes. It's worth seeking the opinions of others, especially if you know that their point of view is sound.

30 FRIDAY
Moon Age Day 21   Moon Sign Leo

The planetary picture provides excellent opportunities for small financial gains, some of which could come like a bolt from the blue. You have potential to outsmart the competition, both at work and in social activities or sports. With the weekend ahead you have an opportunity to pursue a particular idea for having fun.

December
2007

1 SATURDAY
Moon Age Day 22   Moon Sign Virgo

In a social sense you may well be anxious to get some change working in your life. Influences indicate a very restless time for Scorpio, and you may not always feel entirely comfortable with your lot. There are exciting times ahead and you should instinctively realise that this is the case, even if getting things moving takes a while.

2 SUNDAY
Moon Age Day 23   Moon Sign Virgo

Money-making potential reaches a peak around now, motivating you to be far more committed to gaining cash than you are to spending it. Will this cause issues with family members and especially your partner? Well, that all depends on the way you deal with them. You certainly can't afford to look like a Scrooge!

3 MONDAY
Moon Age Day 24   Moon Sign Virgo

Getting some peace and privacy may not be very easy at the moment, particularly if others are calling on your assistance all the time. If it isn't family members who demand your attention it could be friends. You may simply decide not to react however, because basically you need to be needed.

4 TUESDAY
Moon Age Day 25   Moon Sign Libra

Conflicts can arise if you sense that certain people are showing a lack of sensitivity to your own circumstances. Neither will you stand idly by if you think that a friend is being misused in any way. Scorpio's social conscience is extremely heightened under present trends, so why not use this to help yourself and others?

5 WEDNESDAY   *Moon Age Day 26   Moon Sign Libra*

You are now in a position to gain greater control of your personal finances, as well as being able to impose a degree of discipline regarding the spending of others. This is some achievement so close to Christmas, but you should capitalise on good ideas for saving money.

6 THURSDAY   *Moon Age Day 27   Moon Sign Scorpio*

This is a time for grasping nettles firmly, because you have all it takes to be in control of your own destiny. If there is something going on in your life that you don't care for, it's worth sorting it out today and tomorrow. The lunar high enables you to use more luck than usual and even to increase your social standing.

7 FRIDAY   *Moon Age Day 28   Moon Sign Scorpio*

Trends encourage you to show a great deal of faith in the future, both on your own account and in terms of the confidence you have in those around you. You needn't take no for an answer with regard to issues you see as being crucial to your ultimate success, and can afford to put colleagues right if you think their ideas are barmy.

8 SATURDAY   *Moon Age Day 29   Moon Sign Scorpio*

For three days in a row the Moon has been in Scorpio, and although it is losing power now you can still utilise the boost it has given you in order to enjoy Saturday. Now less inclined to think about practical and professional matters, you have scope to have fun, and should have no difficulty enlisting allies.

9 SUNDAY   *Moon Age Day 0   Moon Sign Sagittarius*

This would be a very good time to develop your personal resources and to look towards home-based matters in greater detail. Even if you are more inclined to stay at home than was the case yesterday, you can still find plenty to keep you occupied and it is very unlikely you will be bored.

10 MONDAY *Moon Age Day 1   Moon Sign Sagittarius*

This is another good period during which to get started with financial projects and initiatives. Mercury is in your solar second house, suggesting you should have no difficulty whatsoever in getting your message across, whatever it is. Beware of getting too tied down with pointless red tape or mindless tasks.

11 TUESDAY *Moon Age Day 2   Moon Sign Capricorn*

Your initiative and thinking power remain well starred, and you should know exactly what you want from any given situation, even if others flounder somewhat. You can't expect everyone to keep up with your quick thinking and there are probably going to be times now when you will have to go it alone.

12 WEDNESDAY *Moon Age Day 3   Moon Sign Capricorn*

You are entering a fairly protracted period during which you can ensure that your financial state is slightly better. That's saying something with Christmas just around the corner, but is partly because you are so good at getting a bargain almost everywhere you look. At the same time you may decide to repay debts from the past.

13 THURSDAY *Moon Age Day 4   Moon Sign Capricorn*

This is a day during which you would be wise to avoid getting on the wrong side of others. The fact is that not everyone may be equally easy to either read or to approach. If colleagues especially seem particularly grumpy, this might be a good day to leave them alone. You can approach them better by early next week.

14 FRIDAY *Moon Age Day 5   Moon Sign Aquarius*

Under current influences, financial opportunities and your money sense remain highlighted, and you may find that you are now in a position to command a better salary. Personal incentives are also well accented, and this would be an ideal day to approach a prospective romantic partner.

15 SATURDAY   *Moon Age Day 6   Moon Sign Aquarius*

You cannot afford to remain quiet or to lock yourself away this weekend. Your interests are best served by being out and about, enjoying what life has to offer and also learning more that will be to your own advantage eventually. Rules and regulations can get on your nerves once again, especially if they threaten to mar your weekend.

16 SUNDAY   *Moon Age Day 7   Moon Sign Pisces*

Any Scorpio people who have been rather uptight recently now have scope to loosen up and to express their desires in a better way. You can afford to take time out to be with loved ones and to keep an open attitude to all issues. There are some strange attitudes around, but make sure yours is not one of them!

17 MONDAY   *Moon Age Day 8   Moon Sign Pisces*

Practical affairs have a great deal going for them now, and in terms of money you have potential to make progress. Be prepared to look for genuine bargains as far as those last-minute purchases are concerned, even if that means waiting until even closer to Christmas to get what you are looking for.

18 TUESDAY   *Moon Age Day 9   Moon Sign Aries*

There could be even further gains to be made in the financial sphere, thanks to the present position of the Sun in your solar second house. However, it only stays there for three or four days longer and after that, there's a danger you may decide to spend lavishly. You can find new ways to enjoy yourself tonight.

19 WEDNESDAY   *Moon Age Day 10   Moon Sign Aries*

In your professional and work life you need to be ready to explore new ground, even though Christmas is just around the corner. You can make gains whilst others have taken their eye off the ball, and this is going to be important in the New Year. In a romantic sense you have scope to act on impulse now.

20 THURSDAY
Moon Age Day 11   Moon Sign Taurus

Even if you feel less in charge of your life for the next couple of days, at least you will get the lunar low out of the way before Christmas comes along. Don't be surprised if the last thing you want to do is to go out and have a good time socially. Many Scorpios might simply opt for a warm fire and a good book.

21 FRIDAY
Moon Age Day 12   Moon Sign Taurus

This is a low-key planetary phase and so you may decide that pushing yourself is just a waste of time. What you can do is to look and plan ahead. Your mind remains razor-sharp, and there is little to prevent you from putting matters in hand for projects you know cannot mature for several weeks or even months.

22 SATURDAY
Moon Age Day 13   Moon Sign Gemini

This is a very favourable time for investigations of almost any sort. All the more reason to get your detective head on, as almost anything mysterious could really captivate your attention. Don't be too quick to judge others, especially regarding issues you are not entirely sure about yourself.

23 SUNDAY
Moon Age Day 14   Moon Sign Gemini

Now your mental abilities and your powers of communication are reaching a potential peak. It would take a very good person to fool you in any way and the fact is that you can see through situations as if they were made of glass. New creative pursuits could be on your mind, and these may slightly overtake you.

24 MONDAY
Moon Age Day 15   Moon Sign Cancer

You have scope to make everyday routines a little more interesting and even exciting, though with Christmas only a day away you might be frustrated in some of your practical efforts. Instead of worrying about such things, it would be sensible to simply pitch in and have a good time with your family and friends.

25 TUESDAY   *Moon Age Day 16   Moon Sign Cancer*

You can bring folk round to your way of thinking on this Christmas Day, and you are wonderful at defusing any difficult situation. You can make sure the floor is yours and that everyone wants to listen to what you have to say. Getting to grips with a past family matter might seem a strange way to spend today, but it's certainly an option!

26 WEDNESDAY   *Moon Age Day 17   Moon Sign Leo*

Differences of opinion are possible today, maybe over what you want to do in a social sense. You need to compromise and will have a better time if you are willing to do so. You may decide to travel a short way in order to see someone who lives at a distance or who is rarely at home.

27 THURSDAY   *Moon Age Day 18   Moon Sign Leo*

There is plenty of scope about in terms of new attachments, and even existing relationships are strengthened by present planetary trends. Don't be too quick to apportion blame if something goes slightly wrong. A better response is to pitch in and sort matters out yourself.

28 FRIDAY   *Moon Age Day 19   Moon Sign Leo*

Personal rewards are achievable as a result of your generosity of spirit, which is extremely high at the moment. Mercury gives you even better powers of communication and assists you to form a bridge with someone you haven't always got on well with in the past. You may already be formulating New Year's resolutions, but take it steady!

29 SATURDAY   *Moon Age Day 20   Moon Sign Virgo*

You can make this a busy but nonetheless inspiring time. Whether or not you are actually back at work, you should find plenty to keep you occupied and no lack of incentive when it comes to showing yourself off in social situations. You can persuade everyone to be your friend.

30 SUNDAY   *Moon Age Day 21   Moon Sign Virgo*

Even if you are quite willing to make sacrifices for the sake of friends, beware of letting anyone take advantage of your good nature. This should not be too much of a problem if you are on the ball today and don't allow yourself to be used. Romance looks especially rewarding under present trends.

31 MONDAY   *Moon Age Day 22   Moon Sign Libra*

Attracting the good things in life should be no problem today and you can afford to look ahead towards the New Year in a very progressive manner. It's worth keeping abreast of changes to plans, especially those that mean long-distance travel in a few months. Also stand by for a potentially romantic end to the year.

SCORPIO:
2008 DIARY PAGES

SCORPIO:
2008 IN BRIEF

The start of the year may be quite variable, but the sooner you get on with things, the greater will be your ultimate success. There is no time to either procrastinate or ask too many questions. As a result, January and February work best for you when you take any bull by the horns. Relationships should look especially good, and offer new incentives and a greater confidence in yourself.

As spring arrives, so you will be taking on more in the way of new responsibilities. These don't worry you, and on the contrary this is a time when you can prove a great deal to yourself about your own capabilities. Stand up for your rights and for those of your friends, especially in April. A better time is forecast from a financial point of view and you may have more cash to spare. Personal attachments look good during late April and into the beginning of May.

As May arrives you will be slightly quieter but still capable of getting on well in a general sense. The attitudes of your friends and colleagues vary, so some psychology is necessary on your part. May and June are good for travel, but during both months you need to take opportunities as and when they arise. Waiting around is not to be recommended and you often seem to do best when you are put on the spot.

July and August could turn out to be the best months of the year, but much depends on the way you approach them. The fact is that you need to be confident in your attitude and once you have made up your mind about anything you should stick to it. Once again you will feel the need to travel and to spread your wings in all sorts of ways. A change of job is not out of the question at this time, and taking on new responsibilities will be as easy as falling off a log.

As the autumn arrives, so September and October see you busy assessing your position in life and tinkering with things, maybe more than is strictly necessary. There are down times during both these months and you need to work through issues slowly and methodically in order to sort them out. If you rely heavily on loved ones and friends, you won't be too disappointed with the results.

Have confidence in yourself at the very end of the year and trust to your innate sense of what will work out well. Romance is more definitely highlighted at this time than at any other period during the year and you will be energetic and progressive during both November and December. Christmas should offer you a great deal more than you expect, in terms of both surprises and upward turns in relationships.

January
2008

1 TUESDAY
Moon Age Day 23 Moon Sign Libra

Things may be fairly quiet at the start of the year because just at present you have the Moon in your solar twelfth house. This supports a pensive time when you may be introspective rather than sociable. Making plans could be fun today but putting them into practice is probably best left until Thursday at least.

2 WEDNESDAY
Moon Age Day 24 Moon Sign Libra

Even if you are keeping on the move from a physical standpoint, trends encourage a quieter period than was the case before the turn of the year. With new professional challenges on offer, and many things on your mind, a few hours to contemplate matters would be no bad thing during this interlude.

3 THURSDAY
Moon Age Day 25 Moon Sign Scorpio

Now things really begin to change in a positive way. The Moon moves into your own zodiac sign of Scorpio, that time of the month known as the lunar high. Your energy levels rise and you can show a very confident face to the world at large. Get Lady Luck on your side by all means, though it is your skills that help you the most.

4 FRIDAY
Moon Age Day 26 Moon Sign Scorpio

You have potential to be on top form and to put some of your resolutions into hard and practical action at the end of this first working week of the year. You can persuade colleagues to listen to what you have to say and you can use new possibilities to enhance both your social life and your domestic lot.

5 SATURDAY   *Moon Age Day 27   Moon Sign Sagittarius*

It is towards home and family that your mind is encouraged to turn this weekend and you may decide to spend as much time as possible with your partner or family members. Friends won't be out in the cold but you may be much less inclined to wander far from the walls of your own castle. An introspective phase returns for some.

6 SUNDAY   *Moon Age Day 28   Moon Sign Sagittarius*

Ordinary, everyday talks with people who are familiar to you could carry useful and even important information today. The essential thing is to realise when you are facing a watershed and then how you react to the fact. It might be necessary to leave behind aspects of your life that are now quite clearly redundant.

7 MONDAY   *Moon Age Day 29   Moon Sign Sagittarius*

The Moon is now in your solar third house, helping you to be a good deal more communicative than usual. In particular you can afford to talk about your emotions, possibly to a friend. Spilling the beans in this way allows you to get closer to the way your own inner feelings are running at present.

8 TUESDAY   *Moon Age Day 0   Moon Sign Capricorn*

The Sun is strong in your solar third house and that continues to highlight your communication skills. You know what you want to say and can find new ways of putting across a message that is particularly important to you. Your social conscience is also stimulated by present planetary trends.

9 WEDNESDAY   *Moon Age Day 1   Moon Sign Capricorn*

Make this a light-hearted time and a period during which leisure and pleasure pursuits become ever more important. There's a long way to go before you reach a particular destination that is important to you, but every journey begins with the first step and that is what you should be taking now. Patience works to your advantage at present.

10 THURSDAY   *Moon Age Day 2   Moon Sign Aquarius*

What happens in everyday discussions could be of supreme importance to your future, whether or not you realise the fact at the time. This is why it is vitally important for you to listen carefully and to react only after great thought. In terms of a particular task that you have been set, your best approach is to work slowly towards its conclusion.

11 FRIDAY   *Moon Age Day 3   Moon Sign Aquarius*

Today offers you scope to be the life and soul of any party that takes place in your vicinity, and even to organise one of your own. If there are celebrations somewhere in the family you can be at the heart of them, and family members may be particularly important now.

12 SATURDAY   *Moon Age Day 4   Moon Sign Pisces*

Mars is presently in your solar eighth house and this planetary position can sometimes make possible alterations to your life that you hadn't exactly planned yourself. Something becomes more important and relationships undergo fundamental alterations. Although this can be uncomfortable, you can make sure it turns out for the best.

13 SUNDAY   *Moon Age Day 5   Moon Sign Pisces*

A day to make the most of home and family, though without tying yourself to your living space too much. Despite the fact that the weather is still not good and that winter is all around you, there are times when you need a change of space and new horizons. It's worth getting out of the house in the company of others and having fun.

14 MONDAY   *Moon Age Day 6   Moon Sign Pisces*

Even if you continue to be fairly positive in your attitude, you may not respond well to changes that are imposed upon you, especially at work. The fact is that you want to choose for yourself, and you won't be all that keen to have anyone else telling you what to do. This is not at all unusual for Scorpio, who is very independent.

15 TUESDAY
Moon Age Day 7   Moon Sign Aries

Comfort and security seem to mean very little to you right now, and you may be willing to undergo a good deal of upheaval in order to get something you really want. Once again you can show yourself to be capable of working hard to support other people, and the reforming side of your nature is very much emphasised under present trends.

16 WEDNESDAY
Moon Age Day 8   Moon Sign Aries

There are plenty of rewards available as far as intimate situations are concerned, and it looks as though you can make this one of the most romantic interludes during the whole of January. Any misunderstandings in deep attachments can now be addressed and resolved. Financial matters are also favoured.

17 THURSDAY
Moon Age Day 9   Moon Sign Taurus

Today the Moon arrives at the zodiac sign of Taurus, bringing that part of the month that is known as the lunar low. Taurus is your opposite zodiac sign and with the Moon there you are not encouraged to push yourself, but rather to rest and recharge your batteries. Now is the time for planning rather than doing.

18 FRIDAY
Moon Age Day 10   Moon Sign Taurus

This would be an extremely good day for keeping a generally low profile and for withdrawing from any situations of stress or conflict. Keep a sense of proportion over any issues that are not nearly as important as they first appear. Beware of defending yourself strenuously when you haven't even been attacked in any way.

19 SATURDAY
Moon Age Day 11   Moon Sign Gemini

You now have scope to make things more exciting, and your ability to talk to those around you is much emphasised by the present position of Mercury in your solar chart. You can give yourself fully to new ventures and show a distinctly ingenious streak when it comes to thinking up revolutionary strategies to get things done.

20 SUNDAY   *Moon Age Day 12 Moon Sign Gemini*

Along comes a much more fortunate period from a personal point of view. You have what it takes to express yourself to your partner or sweetheart, and if you are not involved in a personal attachment at the moment, you could find one soon. Routines can be a chore to others today, but not to you.

21 MONDAY   *Moon Age Day 13 Moon Sign Cancer*

Not all influences are positive at the start of this week, and there may be significant challenges being made to your authority. Although this might sometimes bother you it needn't worry you much right now. You can sharpen your intellect in discussions and will usually win out in the end with a mixture of patience and perseverance.

22 TUESDAY   *Moon Age Day 14 Moon Sign Cancer*

Now is the time to show what you are truly made of. Love is important and there isn't much doubt about your ability to attract attention. In some cases an associate or a casual friend can become much more and at the same time you have what it takes to sweep people off their feet. Scorpio is electric now!

23 WEDNESDAY   *Moon Age Day 15 Moon Sign Leo*

Though you can gain a great deal at present by involving yourself in many different tasks and ideas, in the end it's worth focusing on one particular direction. Concentration is important if you want to get ahead in life and there has rarely been a time during which you could focus all your resources more than you can today.

24 THURSDAY   *Moon Age Day 16 Moon Sign Leo*

With Venus in your solar third house you remain very communicative and can use this to strengthen friendships. One person in particular may be figuring in your thinking, and romance is very much to the fore at this stage of the week. Temporary liaisons cannot be ruled out for some Scorpios now.

25 FRIDAY
Moon Age Day 17 Moon Sign Virgo

Getting your own way is now largely a matter of turning on that Scorpio charm. At the same time you can use your magnetic and mysterious nature to become even more attractive than usual. The depth of your thinking is such that very few people can inhabit the world that exists within that fathomless Scorpio mind.

26 SATURDAY
Moon Age Day 18 Moon Sign Virgo

If it seems as though you are hogging the limelight this weekend, you might have to turn down the charisma just a little, though that could be rather hard to achieve under present planetary trends. The fact is that you can now be immensely attractive to others and there may not be a great deal you can do to alter the situation. Would you want to?

27 SUNDAY
Moon Age Day 19 Moon Sign Libra

As the Moon enters your solar twelfth house, you may decide to withdraw into your shell. It isn't that you are upset or miserable, simply that you need time to sort things out and you can't do that when you are constantly in the public eye. Trying to explain your innermost thoughts at present could be very difficult.

28 MONDAY
Moon Age Day 20 Moon Sign Libra

Even if you feel quite practical at the beginning of this week, you might have to rely quite significantly on the good offices of others if you are going to break any records. Nevertheless you can show a strong determination, which gets more obvious with every passing hour. A more potent and successful period is possible just around the corner.

29 TUESDAY ☿
Moon Age Day 21 Moon Sign Libra

Keep watching and planning because the time for concerted action hasn't quite arrived yet. Beware of allowing yourself to get too tied down with details because it is the overview of life that matters the most today. By this evening you can show yourself to be active and enterprising – so much so that you can score a great personal success.

30 WEDNESDAY ☿ *Moon Age Day 22 Moon Sign Scorpio*

You can now take advantage of a physical and mental peak as the Moon arrives in your own zodiac sign of Libra. This is the right time to take all those wonderful ideas and to make them into realities. Doing half a dozen different things at the same time ought to be quite easy, especially if everyone wants to help you.

31 THURSDAY ☿ *Moon Age Day 23 Moon Sign Scorpio*

If ever there was a time to push your luck, you can afford to do so now. Good fortune attends most of your efforts, particularly if you are putting in the right sort of effort in order to get what you want. Insights are particularly good and your ability to see through or around potential obstacles is what really sets you apart today.

February 2008

1 FRIDAY
☿ Moon Age Day 24 Moon Sign Sagittariu

With a great deal of energy still surging through both your mind and body, you needn't settle for second-best in anything. You can show great concern for friends and for people who are not as well off as you are, and may be very charitably minded, both now and across the weekend. All the same, it's worth doing something to please yourself.

2 SATURDAY
☿ Moon Age Day 25 Moon Sign Sagittariu

The Sun presently in your solar fourth house offers a time to think about your family and your home surroundings. It is possible that you will decide to make some sort of change that will make everyone feel more comfortable. Chances are that this will involve an investment of time rather than money.

3 SUNDAY
☿ Moon Age Day 26 Moon Sign Sagittarius

If you have made plans to go anywhere today, be prepared to alter them at the last minute. This doesn't mean that you need to be left out in the cold, or that you will have to make a cancellation. On the contrary, you have what it takes to deal with eventualities as and when they arise. Why not seek the help of friends?

4 MONDAY
☿ Moon Age Day 27 Moon Sign Capricorn

You can make today a pleasant spell at home and a comfortable day during which you don't take on too many pressures. That's fine as far as it goes but some Scorpios might miss the cut and thrust of life, and a few of you may even cause yourself the odd headache – just so you can react!

5 TUESDAY ☿ *Moon Age Day 28 Moon Sign Capricorn*

Your personality is very much to the fore at the moment and you may decide to spend a good deal of today doing things for other people. You tend to be naturally helpful just now and can use your energy to fight for the rights of those you see as being unfairly treated. Scorpio should be especially brave and persevering under present trends.

6 WEDNESDAY ☿ *Moon Age Day 0 Moon Sign Aquarius*

Strong opinions are possible at the moment, and you may be inclined to speak your mind, even when to do so could be against your best interests. It's a good thing therefore that others respect you even more for being honest and it is unlikely that anyone would discriminate against you just because you care.

7 THURSDAY ☿ *Moon Age Day 1 Moon Sign Aquarius*

You can afford to take all opportunities that present themselves today for having a good time – even if to do so might seem slightly selfish in some way. Actually it won't be, particularly if you take others along with you, either in reality or on a mental flight of fancy. At work you can now show your originality.

8 FRIDAY ☿ *Moon Age Day 2 Moon Sign Aquarius*

You can now maximise your potential by paying attention. Nobody can concentrate more or for longer than you and this is a factor that sees you winning through in the end. Whilst others look to short-term gains your mind should be cast way ahead, perhaps even years into the future, though you can also do yourself a lot of good right now.

9 SATURDAY ☿ *Moon Age Day 3 Moon Sign Pisces*

The positive trends continue as far as your home life is concerned and you have scope to contribute heavily to your own happiness and that of family members and friends. As far as romance is concerned, you have what it takes to sweep someone off their feet at the moment – whether it's your long-term lover or not.

81

10 SUNDAY ☿ *Moon Age Day 4 Moon Sign Pisces*

You continue to be quite positive and even a little dominant right now, so much so that you can get people to marvel at your staying power and tenacity. This is not a Sunday for retreating into the background. When the opportunity comes along to shine in a public setting, don't be afraid to turn the switch up fully.

11 MONDAY ☿ *Moon Age Day 5 Moon Sign Aries*

There may be some obstacles about, but you can still move towards your destinations in most areas of life. Working Scorpios could well be especially busy at the start of this week, and this can turn out to be a good thing because there will be a potential lull in a day or two and you need momentum to carry you across it.

12 TUESDAY ☿ *Moon Age Day 6 Moon Sign Aries*

What you can gain from loved ones today should be doubly reassuring and can have a marked bearing on the way you are thinking about life generally. You may be happy to go along with family plans and needn't argue over details you now see as being of no real importance. The same may not be true for everyone!

13 WEDNESDAY ☿ *Moon Age Day 7 Moon Sign Taurus*

The lunar low supports a significantly slower interlude. If you took Old Moore's advice early in the week and gained speed in your actions, you may not notice a sticky patch, but all Scorpios can afford to slow down a little. There could be a few frustrations today, mainly brought about by colleagues.

14 THURSDAY ☿ *Moon Age Day 8 Moon Sign Taurus*

Relationships can be strengthened, but you could falter slightly at work – most likely because of circumstances that are beyond your immediate control. In the main the most significant aspect of the lunar low this month is that it offers few opportunities to speak your mind. You may decide to rely more heavily on others.

15 FRIDAY ☿ *Moon Age Day 9 Moon Sign Gemini*

Your strength lies in recognising a distinct broadening of horizons for both you and those on whom you rely. You can finish the working week with a definite flourish and can do yourself a great deal of good by showing how organised and inventive you can be. Emotions run deep – which is typical for you.

16 SATURDAY ☿ *Moon Age Day 10 Moon Sign Gemini*

Mars remains in your solar eighth house and so change is possible at any stage right now. Some of the alterations could be fundamental, and you seem to know instinctively that you are carrying too much baggage through life. It's time for a very early spring-clean, and this has a bearing on your thinking that proves to be important.

17 SUNDAY ☿ *Moon Age Day 11 Moon Sign Cancer*

Don't be put off today if not everything appears to be going your way. Some inventive thinking may be necessary, and at the same time you can afford to find moments that are filled with nothing but personal happiness. Try to be less of a social reformer for a few hours and relax in good company. Even Scorpio needs a break sometimes.

18 MONDAY ☿ *Moon Age Day 12 Moon Sign Cancer*

There are strong indications that the week ahead can be very important as far as your immediate relationships are concerned. Perhaps you will reach a new understanding with a lover, or it could be that some of your plans for the family are now bearing fruit. At work you have what it takes to be quite ingenious and inventive.

19 TUESDAY ☿ *Moon Age Day 13 Moon Sign Leo*

Even if your practical abilities are considerable at the moment, you may stumble a little when put in a position that means having to speak in public settings. This is probably not because you have any doubt about your subject, but merely because you doubt yourself. You can allow your confidence to grow as the day advances.

20 WEDNESDAY
Moon Age Day 14 Moon Sign Leo

Today offers you scope to contribute heavily to your own success in love and relationships generally. Your magnetic and electric personality can be especially attractive to others at the moment, and you shouldn't have any difficulty impressing anyone. If routines seem a chore, ignore them altogether if you can.

21 THURSDAY
Moon Age Day 15 Moon Sign Leo

Don't expect everyone to agree with you today, particularly if there are people around who will argue that black is white. There is no point at all in trying to bring this type of individual round to your point of view. You would be wise to concentrate your efforts on those individuals who show themselves to be sensible and open-minded.

22 FRIDAY
Moon Age Day 16 Moon Sign Virgo

Progress might be slightly slower than you would wish, though you may be jogging along much more successfully than you believe. You would be wise to avoid family arguments and to stay away from heated discussions that could so easily turn into rows. You need to be sweetness and light today, even if to be so is difficult.

23 SATURDAY
Moon Age Day 17 Moon Sign Virgo

Beware of impulse purchases this weekend, and if possible keep your purse or wallet tightly shut. This is not because you are likely to be duped in any way but merely because the Moon is now in your solar twelfth house. The chance of a genuine bargain could be much greater by the middle of next week, so why not wait a few days?

24 SUNDAY
Moon Age Day 18 Moon Sign Libra

There are some successes possible at present, but these are of a limited nature and you might be best off today simply finding ways to have some fun. It's worth persuading your lover or a close friend to join in with anything that takes your fancy, and all forms of intellectual stimulation appeal to you now.

25 MONDAY
Moon Age Day 19 Moon Sign Libra

This is not a day during which you need to worry much about getting things done quickly. You can afford to be slightly withdrawn, as the real push comes tomorrow. Now is the time to clear the decks for action by getting jobs out of the way that have been hanging around for a while. Be prepared to give help and advice today.

26 TUESDAY
Moon Age Day 20 Moon Sign Scorpio

When it comes to pushing your luck you can get away with almost anything today. An ideal time for shopping, and a period during which you can be very successful in terms of business. Self-employed Scorpio people could be the luckiest of all, particularly if some new form of partnership is presently in the offing.

27 WEDNESDAY
Moon Age Day 21 Moon Sign Scorpio

This is still a very good time for putting new plans into action and for taking elements of the past and remodelling them to suit present circumstances. You can fill yourself with enthusiasm and good ideas. This is something that others recognise and so you should have little or no trouble convincing them of your capabilities.

28 THURSDAY
Moon Age Day 22 Moon Sign Scorpio

You can continue to be quite dynamic and very good to know. Not everyone you meet may be on the same wavelength as you are, which is why you need to discriminate a little at the moment. It is towards the odd or the unusual that your mind is encouraged to turn, and you can find benefits and positive advantages in some unlikely places.

29 FRIDAY
Moon Age Day 23 Moon Sign Sagittarius

The last day of February, even if it is somewhat quieter than the last few days, does have some distinct advantages to offer you. For starters, trends assist you to show off your wits in public settings. When Scorpio hones its communication skills it is a delight to be around. Today also offers new incentives.

March

2008

1 SATURDAY
Moon Age Day 24 Moon Sign Sagittarius

Today can be especially interesting in terms of romance. Maybe it's the arrival of the spring, or the present position of Venus in your solar chart. But for whatever reason you have a chance to prove just how loving and loveable you can be. You can persuade even the most unlikely people to respond to your present warmth.

2 SUNDAY
Moon Age Day 25 Moon Sign Capricorn

You would be wise to look out for minor disagreements that could so easily become something more. You can't really afford to speak your mind with impunity if you want to avoid getting involved in major discussions or arguments. Biting your tongue may not be easier, but it is less difficult than rowing unnecessarily.

3 MONDAY
Moon Age Day 26 Moon Sign Capricorn

You should be able to capitalise on advantages at work and should be doing everything you can to get ahead financially at the moment. However, you needn't worry about cash to the exclusion of everything else because some of the most important gifts that you can attract at the moment do not carry any sort of price tag.

4 TUESDAY
Moon Age Day 27 Moon Sign Capricorn

If you want to show the world who you are and just how capable you can be, be prepared to show off somewhat at this time. There's nothing at all wrong with that, especially bearing in mind all those times when you keep your counsel and say nothing. Even if you shock someone, the result could be far better than you imagine.

5 WEDNESDAY   *Moon Age Day 28 Moon Sign Aquarius*

Certain matters can be brought to a head in professional matters, and you would be well advised to keep your wits about you when at work. You need to respond quickly and positively to changing circumstances and should not leave anything to chance. Taking command is something you understand, even if you do so quietly and without fuss.

6 THURSDAY   *Moon Age Day 29 Moon Sign Aquarius*

This is a time to be as creative as you can possibly manage. New hobbies are possible, and you can afford to change aspects of your life that are not going in quite the way you would have wished. There are times when you simply have to go with the flow, but today is probably not one of them.

7 FRIDAY   *Moon Age Day 0 Moon Sign Pisces*

A day to make an early start with all tasks and duties – that way you will leave yourself more time later for personal enjoyment. You have scope to find things to captivate your imagination, and some interesting people may well emerge around now. Beware of getting tied down with pointless rules and regulations today.

8 SATURDAY   *Moon Age Day 1 Moon Sign Pisces*

Work and practical progress should be easy enough, leaving you with more hours to please yourself. It may only now have occurred to you that the seasons are changing, and you could benefit greatly from getting out of the house and simply taking a walk. Rather than being on your own too much today, why not stick with friends?

9 SUNDAY   *Moon Age Day 2 Moon Sign Aries*

Someone you don't see too often could well make an appearance around now and could bring with them memories of the past that are strong and emotional. Today offers all sorts of practical incentives, but it is just possible that you will fail to address some of these if your mind is too closely focused on things that happened years ago.

10 MONDAY   *Moon Age Day 3   Moon Sign Aries*

Trends assist you to be fairly sure of yourself today, but this is not a situation that will last for too long. The lunar low is on the way and you would be wise to protect yourself by making your position in life as solid as you can. It's worth letting others know the way you feel about specific matters and getting any important jobs out of the way.

11 TUESDAY   *Moon Age Day 4   Moon Sign Taurus*

A quieter time is possible, and you may not have all that much influence over life generally. For that reason you may decide to have a well-earned rest, whilst others take some of the strain. Even if your attitude is one of some resignation at the moment, it won't be long before you can get back in harness and make a bigger impression.

12 WEDNESDAY   *Moon Age Day 5   Moon Sign Taurus*

This is hardly the best time to be overconfident and it would be wise to check and double-check details. This is particularly true with regard to travel, either now or in the near future. Why not use some of your spare time today to catch up socially with people you don't see as often as you might wish? Relatives might be somewhat demanding.

13 THURSDAY   *Moon Age Day 6   Moon Sign Gemini*

Opportunities for excitement are available, and at least some of them have to do with movement in your life generally. If there are journeys on offer you should grab such chances as confidently and quickly as you can. Now is the time to support friends with schemes you see as being both honourable and potentially rewarding.

14 FRIDAY   *Moon Age Day 7   Moon Sign Gemini*

Mercury is now entering your solar fourth house, assisting you to make communications between yourself and family members much easier and somewhat more comfortable than they may have been of late. If younger or capricious relatives make a splash, you should be especially pleased to congratulate them.

15 SATURDAY
Moon Age Day 8 Moon Sign Cancer

The atmosphere in your life generally could perhaps best be described as one of anticipation. There is plenty that you want to do, and many opportunities that seem to be on offer, yet the time may not be quite right to act. You can best curb any impatience this weekend by finding something to do that is enjoyable and which pleases your partner.

16 SUNDAY
Moon Age Day 9 Moon Sign Cancer

Weekend-working Scorpios have much to look forward to on this particular Sunday, though if you are at leisure today you will have to make up your own mind about what you want to do. Even if you still feel as if you are in life's waiting room, you can change things quite dramatically once the new working week gets started.

17 MONDAY
Moon Age Day 10 Moon Sign Cancer

It's possible that you might have to put in extra hours this week as far as your work is concerned, but the progress you can make as a result shows that the effort is well worthwhile. It is towards the material side of life that your mind is now encouraged to turn, and you might even decide not to socialise until later in the week.

18 TUESDAY
Moon Age Day 11 Moon Sign Leo

The time is right to go after a number of personal objectives and to put the finishing touches to any jobs that have been ongoing for quite some time. Trends support a feeling that everything is about to change, and although this can make you quite nervy in some ways, the potential excitement is tantalising.

19 WEDNESDAY
Moon Age Day 12 Moon Sign Leo

Some impatience is now possible, as indeed has been the case for a number of days now. This is especially true in professional matters, though you can also push on towards new possibilities when away from the sphere of work. It is still those final little details that get in the way, and your patience is far from assured.

20 THURSDAY *Moon Age Day 13 Moon Sign Virgo*

The very practical aspects of life are now highlighted, and you have scope to find plenty of assistance at the moment if you need it. You might not be quite as tolerant of others as would sometimes be the case, particularly if you are dealing with people who simply won't use any common sense.

21 FRIDAY *Moon Age Day 14 Moon Sign Virgo*

This is not a day during which you should believe everything you hear. Beware of potential bargains that will turn out to be anything but, and at the same time keep a careful watch on your finances. A little suspicion would be no bad thing for Scorpio at the moment.

22 SATURDAY *Moon Age Day 15 Moon Sign Libra*

The means to build on recent successes is all around you but it takes a very original view of life to fully appreciate the fact. In some ways you can be quite ingenious at the moment and needn't be afraid to use unconventional means in order to get your way. It's worth seeking support from friends.

23 SUNDAY *Moon Age Day 16 Moon Sign Libra*

Most of the positive highlights that crop up at the moment relate to your social life, despite the fact that a twelfth-house Moon encourages a somewhat quieter time than would sometimes be the case. Setting yourself mental tasks could be fun, and you can afford to test yourself in many different ways under present planetary trends.

24 MONDAY *Moon Age Day 17 Moon Sign Libra*

An ideal day to get together with friends and discover new ways to have fun. You should also make the most of the time of year because it should be more than obvious to you now that the worst of winter is finished and the spring is poised to lighten your life. Some of the darkness at the heart of the Scorpio nature can now be blown away

25 TUESDAY
Moon Age Day 18 Moon Sign Scorpio

This is the best time of the month to get new plans underway and to think up strategies that may have been out of the question for a while. You can make the most of your energy and a great wish to achieve your heart's desire. Best of all, you can end the period of waiting that typified the last week or two.

26 WEDNESDAY
Moon Age Day 19 Moon Sign Scorpio

Be prepared to marshal all of your energy into one very definite plan of action because the lunar high supports success. In a social and a romantic sense you can make sure that you are flavour of the month, and your general popularity is inclined to go from strength to strength. New romance is possible for some.

27 THURSDAY
Moon Age Day 20 Moon Sign Sagittarius

You have what it takes to be forceful and determined, but you might have to move with just a little caution, especially if you are dealing with people who are hesitant or nervy by nature. Not everyone might have either your fortitude or your conviction, and this period of absolute certainty you are going through could startle others!

28 FRIDAY
Moon Age Day 21 Moon Sign Sagittarius

There is little doubt that you can put yourself on a winning streak in a professional sense and also get a lot out of your social life. Most important of all will be your attitude towards romance. If you are not involved in a specific attachment at the moment, it's worth paying attention because there are possibilities.

29 SATURDAY
Moon Age Day 22 Moon Sign Sagittarius

A little peace and quiet – which in some ways appears to be quite inviting – may not be possible under present trends. On the contrary, you could be in great demand from both family members and friends. Trying to find moments to please yourself might mean having to disappoint someone – and you don't want that.

30 SUNDAY   *Moon Age Day 23 Moon Sign Capricorn*

A trend is now underway that throws favourable highlights on all relationship issues. This is most obvious when it comes to deep, emotional attachments. Things go better in twosomes, and you can afford to be attentive and romantic. In most settings today you are inclined to act almost totally on impulse.

31 MONDAY   *Moon Age Day 24 Moon Sign Capricorn*

You have what it takes to make the tide of fortune flow in your direction, and to do this without any tangible effort. Practical common sense makes it easy for you to steer a path between potential obstacles, whilst at the same time you can be so charming that nobody would refuse any reasonable request. Money matters can be strengthened.

April

2008

1 TUESDAY
Moon Age Day 25 Moon Sign Aquarius

Your competitive drive continues to allow you the sort of progress that was harder to achieve earlier in the year. Physical energy is highlighted, assisting you to become ever more competitive. In sporting activities your efforts are well starred, and you also have a great ability to mix business with pleasure this week.

2 WEDNESDAY
Moon Age Day 26 Moon Sign Aquarius

Even if working hard is the last thing on your mind, you might still manage to get a great deal done. The fact is that for today at least you have scope to have fun but on the way you can show yourself to be both capable and captivating to others. This fascinating phase should not be lost on friends.

3 THURSDAY
Moon Age Day 27 Moon Sign Pisces

You now have scope to reap positive results from your recent efforts. It might be best to deliberately slow your pace in some areas, and this is very true at work. Consolidate on present gains before pushing forward, and allow yourself to enjoy the fruits of your successes for a day or two.

4 FRIDAY
Moon Age Day 28 Moon Sign Pisces

Your strength lies in gaining support and attention from those close to you. There is so much love and affection around you at the moment that it sometimes gets difficult to concentrate on the strictly routine and practical in life. The potential for the weekend is good, so why not get together with your pals to plan something special?

5 SATURDAY
Moon Age Day 29 Moon Sign Pisces

Trends suggest a desire to get involved with others today, and you may not be happy if you have to spend protracted periods of time on your own. If you have made progress of late, you can now afford to have fun. Any sort of short journey might be especially attractive – and the more so if you are in good company.

6 SUNDAY
Moon Age Day 0 Moon Sign Aries

Intimate attachments could prove to be quite demanding today, at a time when you really want to mix as freely as possible. It's worth avoiding any intense situations and people who are over-emotional. For once Scorpio is happy to graze the surface of life and to simply see situations for what they appear to be.

7 MONDAY
Moon Age Day 1 Moon Sign Aries

Intimate relationships could prove to be rather demanding this week and you would be wise to ring the changes a little and to get away from the intensity by concentrating on more casual attachments too. Scorpio does tend to smoulder a great deal in an emotional sense and there are times when a lighter touch works its own magic.

8 TUESDAY
Moon Age Day 2 Moon Sign Taurus

This is definitely a favourable time to involve yourself in new ideas, though with the lunar low around you may decide to do little more than plan your strategies. If you get too tied up with jobs at a physical level you will soon tire yourself out. Better by far for the moment to allow others to do the work, whilst you supervise.

9 WEDNESDAY
Moon Age Day 3 Moon Sign Taurus

Independent efforts are not as well accented at the moment as co-operative ventures. This is partly because of the lunar low but also on account of your need of reassurance and support. To others you often seem to be overflowing with confidence and quite able to stand alone, but at its core Scorpio is rarely as positive as it looks.

10 THURSDAY
Moon Age Day 4 Moon Sign Gemini

There could be new social highlights in the offing, and today is a good day to look for these. Don't allow an opportunity to have fun to pass you by, simply because you are tied down with all sorts of routines. Be willing to look at things from a different point of view, and seek the advice of friends.

11 FRIDAY
Moon Age Day 5 Moon Sign Gemini

Trends support a warm-hearted and very soft response to family members but also to strangers. This is the kind side of Scorpio and is particularly favoured at the moment because your social-reforming impulses are much aroused. You have scope to help anyone who is less well off or confident than you presently are.

12 SATURDAY
Moon Age Day 6 Moon Sign Cancer

Why not maximise your potential today by being more organised? You can get a great deal done and still have time to enjoy yourself, but not unless you plan things properly first. There is no point at all in trying to do half a dozen different things at the same time, because this could well cause a good deal of confusion and replication.

13 SUNDAY
Moon Age Day 7 Moon Sign Cancer

Intimate encounters are well starred on this April Sunday and it looks as though you have what it takes to make the best possible impression on people who have only recently come into your life. Your sporting instincts are aroused, enabling you to show a strong competitive edge that may well assure you of a personal victory.

14 MONDAY
Moon Age Day 8 Moon Sign Leo

If you can keep relationships quite harmonious at the moment, you shouldn't be diverted by the usual worries regarding family members. On the contrary, much of what you do can be focused on the wider world outside your own front door. Getting together with colleagues can see new ideas positively forging ahead.

15 TUESDAY
Moon Age Day 9 Moon Sign Leo

The present position of the Moon helps you to make your social life more interesting and stimulates your curiosity. You want to turn over every stone that you encounter on your path through life, just to see what might be beneath it. In company you show tact and diplomacy to such an extent that you can persuade everyone to confide in you.

16 WEDNESDAY
Moon Age Day 10 Moon Sign Virgo

Romantic feelings towards others are to the fore, and this might turn out to be one of the most interesting periods of April as far as intimate attachments are concerned. Scorpio simmers with emotion, and can also find the right words to make that most important person love you all the more. It's worth protecting financial interests.

17 THURSDAY
Moon Age Day 11 Moon Sign Virgo

Your mind may now be slightly less focused, and you gain most by taking a broad overview of life. If you concentrate too much on any one issue you could get to a position from which it is impossible to see the wood for the trees. Better by far at the moment to spread your interests and to take a little from many different influences.

18 FRIDAY
Moon Age Day 12 Moon Sign Libra

Relationships continue to bring out the best in you, and despite a potential desire to get on in a material sense, it is towards your personal life that trends encourage you to turn more and more. However, this need not prevent you from planning ahead, especially where travel is concerned. You now have what it takes to invest wisely.

19 SATURDAY
Moon Age Day 13 Moon Sign Libra

Don't be afraid to focus on fun and games this weekend, though in a way that doesn't demand too much in the way of energy. With the Moon in your solar twelfth house you may be slightly quieter and just a little more introspective, though still carrying a desire to enjoy yourself. It's worth listening to the ideas of friends at the moment.

20 SUNDAY
Moon Age Day 14 Moon Sign Libra

That twelfth-house Moon encourages a quieter period, but there are great times ahead and a little prior planning might prove to be advantageous. The attitude of family members needs some careful thinking about during today, and a good deal of your time may be given over to ensuring that everyone has what they need to get on.

21 MONDAY
Moon Age Day 15 Moon Sign Scorpio

With the lunar high comes a period during which you can afford to take a few more risks than has been possible so far this month. You have the ability to get ahead without trying too hard, which leaves time and incentive for new ideas and revised strategies. Others should have your best interests at heart.

22 TUESDAY
Moon Age Day 16 Moon Sign Scorpio

Energy remains in good supply and you can use it to forge ahead with your own desires and dreams. What an excellent time this would be for travel and for meeting all manner of people who inspire you. There may be disruptions that have to be dealt with, but that's generally a good thing for Scorpio and prevents you from getting in a rut.

23 WEDNESDAY
Moon Age Day 17 Moon Sign Sagittarius

Make the most of your ability to get to the core of the thought processes of your relatives and friends. You may be especially aware of opportunities to make progress in a material sense, but might also be quite busy organising the lives of people who really need your special touch. Today could be exhausting but also rewarding.

24 THURSDAY
Moon Age Day 18 Moon Sign Sagittarius

It is possible that you will encounter disputes of one sort or another today, even if you are not the person who is promoting them. Your services as an arbitrator can be used to sort everyone out – whilst avoiding getting too involved yourself. Scorpio walks a fine line today, but can do so admirably.

25 FRIDAY
Moon Age Day 19 Moon Sign Sagittarius

Interactions with colleagues and friends are best kept free from any sort of complications, and life should be as simple as it can be. This is especially good for Scorpio, which always seems to be in the midst of one intrigue or another. For once you needn't get involved in secrets – either your own or those of people around you.

26 SATURDAY
Moon Age Day 20 Moon Sign Capricorn

If you make sure you get on well with everyone, your popularity should be rising rapidly. In the main you are still straightforward in your attitude and will not be in the market for duplicity. Being scrupulously honest is the best policy and can pay handsome dividends further down the road. A day to seek new friends.

27 SUNDAY
Moon Age Day 21 Moon Sign Capricorn

The sense of responsibility you feel towards others could easily get in the way of your own desires today, but as is usually the case for Scorpio, duty comes first. It would be very wise to seek the help and support of people who have particular skills, and to realise that you can't solve all potential problems yourself.

28 MONDAY
Moon Age Day 22 Moon Sign Aquarius

The present position of Venus in your solar chart assists you to be very much in tune with others and also with yourself. This is not usually the case, because you are given to periods of self-doubt and anxiety. For the moment you can afford to be extremely confident and happy to live the simplest of lives.

29 TUESDAY
Moon Age Day 23 Moon Sign Aquarius

Intimacy with a loved one can now transcend usual boundaries, and you can achieve a 'oneness' that often escapes you. This is because you are less locked inside your own deep nature. You show a freshness and a natural vitality that is very attractive to others. In a professional sense you should be on a roll at the moment.

30 WEDNESDAY   *Moon Age Day 24   Moon Sign Aquarius*

Whether at work or at home you would be wise not to take anything for granted. Although there could be a few setbacks at the moment, you have what it takes to get on well and to deal with eventualities as and when they arise. A day to avoid trying to solve problems that probably don't even exist, and to be as discriminating as possible.

2008

1 THURSDAY
Moon Age Day 25 Moon Sign Pisces

Subtle changes in the nature of events can make your goals and objectives less certain at the moment. That is why it might be best to pause, whilst you look at many matters slightly differently. There isn't much point in ploughing on regardless because this could result in you having to do things again. Why not seek support from friends?

2 FRIDAY
Moon Age Day 26 Moon Sign Pisces

Your ambitions are enhanced, and despite any remaining confusion at the heart of your life, you can look at most matters in a very philosophical way. You might be especially good at problem-solving right now, and should revel in any sort of puzzle – most of which are undertaken simply because it amuses you.

3 SATURDAY
Moon Age Day 27 Moon Sign Aries

Old patterns of thinking could now break down slightly, and you could stumble under the weight of responsibilities. Some of these are far less onerous than you think and in any case there is always help and support around if you choose to look for it. Be prepared to welcome back someone you haven't seen for ages.

4 SUNDAY
Moon Age Day 28 Moon Sign Aries

Avoid getting tense about issues that are not really your responsibility. There is sometimes a tendency for Scorpio to get itself involved in matters that are beyond its remit and which can only be sorted out by others. All you achieve by doing so is to confuse your own life and to waste valuable time. Be very discriminating today.

5 MONDAY
Moon Age Day 0 Moon Sign Taurus

A significant influx of new ideas is possible this week, but there may be very little you can do about them until the middle of the week. With the lunar low around you may decide to withdraw into yourself, and won't be at all inclined to push yourself beyond certain specified limits. However you can still be very affectionate.

6 TUESDAY
Moon Age Day 1 Moon Sign Taurus

Mundane tasks may well seem to be more trouble than they are worth, and trends don't assist with any significant headway for the moment. It would probably be best not to bother for now and instead you need to allow others to take the strain and to help you out when necessary. Don't let pride get in your way at present.

7 WEDNESDAY
Moon Age Day 2 Moon Sign Gemini

Certain desires can now be met more successfully than would have been the case on Monday or Tuesday, but it could take you a few hours today to get up to speed. In particular you are in a position to do especially well in all co-operative ventures and where your unique and sometimes off-the-wall ideas are of great value.

8 THURSDAY
Moon Age Day 3 Moon Sign Gemini

The present position of Mars could bring a slightly tense atmosphere to personal attachments, which your present attitude may make worse. Try to be as relaxed as possible today and allow any chance remarks to go over your head. You might be too sensitive for your own good now.

9 FRIDAY
Moon Age Day 4 Moon Sign Cancer

Your intuition is fairly strong, except when you are dealing with matters that have a bearing on your own personal or romantic life. When it comes to assessing others and situations beyond your own life you can be excellent. Don't be surprised if people naturally turn to you for help and advice today, and be ready to do what you can.

101

10 SATURDAY *Moon Age Day 5 Moon Sign Cancer*

A period of significant change is now on offer, and this could mean 'out with the old and in with the new'. Although planetary trends are good, it may be hard to part with certain aspects of the past, if only because of your nostalgic turn of mind. Your strength lies in recognising that you sometimes carry too much luggage.

11 SUNDAY *Moon Age Day 6 Moon Sign Leo*

You have scope to find plenty of contentment today if you spend as much time as possible with friends. Don't do anything particularly unusual but stick to what you know and like. There should be opportunities to move around a good deal and any sort of journey, whether it has been planned for weeks or not, should benefit you.

12 MONDAY *Moon Age Day 7 Moon Sign Leo*

Conversations with your partner or sweetheart may well be on the cards for today. It's worth finding sufficient time to talk at length and not crowding your schedule today with all sorts of tasks that have no real significance. You might have to be especially discriminating at work and this could mean disappointing someone.

13 TUESDAY *Moon Age Day 8 Moon Sign Virgo*

Some matters could prove to be quite tiresome today, and you probably won't want to talk for hours on end to people who seem to have nothing sensible to say. In addition, it could seem that you are spending valuable hours doing things you know are a waste of time. With this regard at least, a rethink might be in order later in the day.

14 WEDNESDAY *Moon Age Day 9 Moon Sign Virgo*

Stand by for a period of inner reflection. Today responds best if you spend at least some time on your own and don't get involved too much in projects that are not of your own invention. Whilst some might accuse you of being selfish, it is nevertheless important to do what seems right to you personally.

15 THURSDAY   *Moon Age Day 10 Moon Sign Virgo*

There are small gains to be made today, and even if none of these seem especially important in themselves they could begin to add up as the day wears on. Attitude is very important when it comes to a professional offer that might be on the table. This could be a sideways move of some sort, but it may have its benefits.

16 FRIDAY   *Moon Age Day 11 Moon Sign Libra*

You can afford to be more trusting at the moment. There is nothing at all unusual about this state of affairs because Scorpio is often rather sceptical and rarely considers that anyone does anything for selfless reasons. Suspicion is the hallmark of your zodiac sign, but it might be slightly too prevalent under present planetary trends.

17 SATURDAY   *Moon Age Day 12 Moon Sign Libra*

Keep up your efforts to forge ahead because although the weekend might mean there is little progress to be made as far as work is concerned, your mind can work overtime and help you to see your way ahead. At the same time you need to have fun today and to spend as many hours as possible with loved ones.

18 SUNDAY   *Moon Age Day 13 Moon Sign Scorpio*

It's worth getting ahead as quickly as you can with important dreams and schemes. The lunar high allows you to get something you really want, even if you have to put in significant effort to do so. Energy levels are off the scale and you should be more than happy to test yourself both physically and mentally whilst the Moon remains in Scorpio.

19 MONDAY   *Moon Age Day 14 Moon Sign Scorpio*

It would be very worthwhile to trust your hunches at the start of this particular week. You can get things working well for you and there is a strong indication that a combination of natural luck and pure common sense are going to favour most of your efforts. It's time to see the path to the future as clearly as if you were walking it now.

20 TUESDAY *Moon Age Day 15 Moon Sign Scorpio*

For the third day in a row the Moon remains in Scorpio and brings a high element of luck to most of your endeavours. Translated into everyday life this helps you to make sure your efforts work out first time, so that repeating yourself is very unlikely. You can attract words of affection from surprising directions.

21 WEDNESDAY *Moon Age Day 16 Moon Sign Sagittarius*

Stand by to make this a fairly productive period as far as money is concerned. It isn't that there is more cash about than you might expect but the fact is that you can use what you have more effectively. Attention to detail is very important when you are at work, and it is essential that you go on getting things right first time every time.

22 THURSDAY *Moon Age Day 17 Moon Sign Sagittarius*

You can widen your horizons under present trends, and can get on especially well with people who are naturally optimistic and dynamic by nature. You would be wise to leave alone those individuals whose presence in your life is a drain on your physical and mental resources. You may need to be firm with a family member.

23 FRIDAY *Moon Age Day 18 Moon Sign Capricorn*

If you are finding it somewhat difficult to compromise right now, you may have to work that much harder in order to find solutions to personal disagreements. As long as you realise that you could be rather unreasonable there is something you can do about the situation. The real problem only comes if you refuse to recognise your own nature.

24 SATURDAY *Moon Age Day 19 Moon Sign Capricorn*

Travel and getting about generally are highlighted at the moment, and the weekend ought to offer you quite a few opportunities to do something different. Even if part of you wants to follow the same old routines, you would be wise to realise that change and diversity are essential as well. Friends can seem rather pushy.

25 SUNDAY   *Moon Age Day 20 Moon Sign Capricorn*

Trends encourage you to express yourself, and you have what it takes to make significant progress, especially in personal matters. Joining forces with friends could be fun at the moment and especially so if you do something that is completely different and which taxes you physically or mentally.

26 MONDAY   *Moon Age Day 21 Moon Sign Aquarius*

You can afford to show others your sociable and charming side for the first part of this week. This means you are in an ideal position to chase something you have wanted for ages. You can make sure that people who are in the best possible position to do you some good are looking at you in a very positive way right now.

27 TUESDAY   ☿ *Moon Age Day 22 Moon Sign Aquarius*

Get out and see what is happening on the social scene today, and don't get so bogged down with work that you fail to put aside any time to simply be yourself. If friends and relatives are trying to involve you in things they have planned, it should be possible for you to join in at some stage.

28 WEDNESDAY ☿   *Moon Age Day 23 Moon Sign Pisces*

There should now be a significant opportunity to get a backlog of work cleared up – even if you have to bully other people into helping you. There are gains to be made on the financial front, particularly if you use your organisational skills, but you should also be able to harness some significant luck at present.

29 THURSDAY   ☿   *Moon Age Day 24 Moon Sign Pisces*

This is an ideal time during which to explore your own horizons and a period to consider your capabilities. You may have spent months or even years educating yourself in some way and it looks as though the circumstances are now right to show what you have learned. Look out for more financial gains and exploit new starts.

30 FRIDAY ☿ *Moon Age Day 25 Moon Sign Aries*

You still have scope to act on impulse and to leave behind that less than positive and suspicious quality that lies at the heart of Scorpio. Physical activity is favoured at the moment, and you needn't be held back by the sort of situation that sometimes hampers you. On the contrary, you should positively welcome most challenges.

31 SATURDAY ☿ *Moon Age Day 26 Moon Sign Aries*

Some aspects of life might seem strange or even weird today, but you can deal with these quite easily. In particular you may decide to tackle family members or friends who are behaving in the most odd ways, which might lead you to believe they are hiding something. This can be frustrating because you hate secrets – except your own!

June

2008

1 SUNDAY ☿ *Moon Age Day 27 Moon Sign Taurus*

Your confidence is not favoured today, and you might have to settle for second-best – if only for a day or two. The lunar low doesn't enhance your present vitality and there is now more of a tendency for you to sit for ages in your favourite chair. Even when you are relaxing there is nothing to prevent you from planning things.

2 MONDAY ☿ *Moon Age Day 28 Moon Sign Taurus*

A personal issue could get in the way of your progress in a general sense today, particularly if you let it dominate your mind. The lunar low encourages you to dwell on things, sometimes without any real cause. Try to be as optimistic as possible and don't turn down the chance of some real assistance.

3 TUESDAY ☿ *Moon Age Day 29 Moon Sign Gemini*

If you are involved in group activities today, you have what it takes to put yourself in charge. Scorpio doesn't take kindly to being told what to do, but what is really called for at the moment is genuine co-operation. If you pool your ideas, listening as much as you are talking, the result should turn out to be that much better.

4 WEDNESDAY ☿ *Moon Age Day 0 Moon Sign Gemini*

Why not try for a change of scenery today? You could easily get tired if you are forced to look at the same four walls, and although a degree of effort may be required to get away from routines, the result could more than repay you. It's worth taking friends with you on your journeys – even if these turn out to be merely flights of fancy.

5 THURSDAY ☿ *Moon Age Day 1 Moon Sign Cancer*

There is more than enough pressure in your life to be going on with for the moment. Try to be bold in your strategies but also check details before getting involved in any sort of risky venture. On the whole it might be best at the moment to stick to what you know. The best time for taking chances lies in the future, beyond the next few days.

6 FRIDAY ☿ *Moon Age Day 2 Moon Sign Cancer*

Trends suggest you may be slightly uncomfortable in social settings today and across the weekend. This could be for no other reason than your naturally tendency to doubt your own abilities. Look in a mirror and tell yourself that you are fascinating to know and that people find you captivating. This is no lie, so believe it!

7 SATURDAY ☿ *Moon Age Day 3 Moon Sign Leo*

You can now find the inspiration to spread your wings, and some Scorpio people may be thinking seriously about changes at home. A house move could even be in the offing and although there is a certain amount of nostalgia to hold you back, the thought of better times to come and greater comfort could be the deciding factor.

8 SUNDAY ☿ *Moon Age Day 4 Moon Sign Leo*

Beware of allowing social events to turn into the 'same old thing'. No matter how much personal effort you have to put in it is worthwhile to shake things up a little. Not everyone will be equally helpful today and it is sensible to stick to those people who have always been reliable and who don't tend to change their minds regularly.

9 MONDAY ☿ *Moon Age Day 5 Moon Sign Leo*

If you seek out people who help you to broaden your perspectives, you could well be in for a busy week. You would be wise to keep finances at the forefront of your thinking, and there will be plenty to keep your mind occupied. Leave some time free for simple enjoyment along with your friends.

10 TUESDAY ☿ *Moon Age Day 6 Moon Sign Virgo*

Look out for an emphasis on personal concerns. Maybe your love life has not been going quite according to plan, or it could seem that someone you care for deeply has gone slightly cold on you. Your anxiety might be misplaced, and if you do a little digging you should be able to discover what is really going on.

11 WEDNESDAY ☿ *Moon Age Day 7 Moon Sign Virgo*

A day to keep up your striving for change and variety because this will prevent you from feeling slightly lacking in vitality. Even if you can't do everything you want in a physical or a material sense for the next couple of days, you can think and plan. By Saturday you should be in a position to turn ideas into realities.

12 THURSDAY ☿ *Moon Age Day 8 Moon Sign Libra*

A quieter period is now possible, thanks to the position of the Moon, which now occupies your solar twelfth house. You could still be contemplative and inclined to spend at least some time on your own. What you don't need is to worry about situations over which you have little or no control.

13 FRIDAY ☿ *Moon Age Day 9 Moon Sign Libra*

The signs are that not everything that occurs to you as being a good idea is going to be popular with those around you. You might have to do a good deal of persuading if you want life to go the way you would wish. In some cases it might be better simply to follow your own course and to allow others to do the same.

14 SATURDAY ☿ *Moon Age Day 10 Moon Sign Scorpio*

With the weekend comes the lunar high, offering you a chance to put all those thoughts that you have been mulling over during the week to the test. You can make an impression on others and should be showing the most social face so far this month. There's a good chance that certain other people will find you very attractive now.

15 SUNDAY ☿ *Moon Age Day 11 Moon Sign Scorpio*

Keeping up a high profile really will work at the moment and there is nothing half so good as feeling that you can get people to listen to what you have to say. As the year advances so you feel more and more like travel and everything is set fair for you to make a journey that might have been on your mind ever since the winter.

16 MONDAY ☿ *Moon Age Day 12 Moon Sign Scorpio*

This is another favourable day for getting your own way. You can redress the balance at work by persuading anyone who was sceptical about your ideas last week to show you the most support. Don't be in the least frightened to air your views, even to bosses or people with real power.

17 TUESDAY ☿ *Moon Age Day 13 Moon Sign Sagittarius*

You should do everything you can at the moment to ensure that you come across to others in a dynamic and very positive way. This can't be achieved by hiding your light under a bushel, so you are simply going to have to show what you are made of. Once you get over your initial nerves there is very little that is presently beyond you.

18 WEDNESDAY ☿ *Moon Age Day 14 Moon Sign Sagittarius*

Today has potential to be refreshing and inspiring in a social sense and should continue to allow you to make progress in a professional sense too. Once material and practical considerations are out of the way, it's worth finding time to concentrate on your personal life. Try a few compliments and watch your sweetheart melt!

19 THURSDAY ☿ *Moon Age Day 15 Moon Sign Capricorn*

Certain emotions remain very close to the surface, and even if you haven't really thought about the situation, today offers a chance to rebuild aspects of your romantic life. Maybe things have been a little dull of late in that area of your life, but you can certainly make a difference right now.

20 FRIDAY ☿ *Moon Age Day 16 Moon Sign Capricorn*

A day to gain stimulation from others, which allows you to turn up the power of your own charisma too. Make sure you get plenty of fresh air and exercise at the moment because your general state of mind is now tied specifically to the way you treat your body. Don't allow yourself to become in the least sluggish, and eat sensibly.

21 SATURDAY *Moon Age Day 17 Moon Sign Capricorn*

If what you are really looking for at the moment is personal freedom, it is just possible that events surrounding you this weekend will make that possible. Now is the time to drop all negative thoughts and occupy your mind with what you 'can' do. Why not seek support from friends?

22 SUNDAY *Moon Age Day 18 Moon Sign Aquarius*

Being a Water sign, there are times when Scorpio thinks it makes very little difference to anything. This is the negative side of your mind, but there is no place for it under present planetary trends. Now you should realise just how much you can achieve, and can afford to move heaven and earth in order to get somewhere you really want to be.

23 MONDAY *Moon Age Day 19 Moon Sign Aquarius*

Rather than being kept down this week, be prepared to make sure that everyone is aware of your presence and your excellent ideas. Money matters should be easier to cope with and you could even discover that you are slightly better off than you expected to be. A day to leave boring jobs for others and find new interests yourself.

24 TUESDAY *Moon Age Day 20 Moon Sign Pisces*

It is true that you get out of life what you are willing to put in, which is why you can get so much working to your advantage under present trends. Even minor jobs at work can bring significant rewards, and once you are free to do what you want, you might decide to try new sporting activities or pursuits that feed your intellectual side.

25 WEDNESDAY *Moon Age Day 21 Moon Sign Pisces*

Now the opportunities that stand before you are major in proportion and there won't be a better time during June to achieve something that you have been wanting for a very long time. This demands a certain degree of courage and you should not be lacking in that department. You can impress others with your fortitude and determination.

26 THURSDAY *Moon Age Day 22 Moon Sign Pisces*

Trends suggest a slight impulsiveness, and you would be wise to check and recheck details before you take on anything new or revolutionary. It isn't that life is working against you – merely that you may be trying too hard. Be prepared to turn down your rash side a little, in favour of some practical common sense.

27 FRIDAY *Moon Age Day 23 Moon Sign Aries*

Make an early start and get all unfinished jobs out of the way ahead of the weekend. It would be better if there were nothing to cloud your horizons for tomorrow, leaving you completely free to follow your own whims. From a social point of view you can paint the town red this evening, so contacting a few friends would be no bad thing.

28 SATURDAY *Moon Age Day 24 Moon Sign Aries*

Once again you can be a creature of the moment, though by tomorrow the situation changes markedly so you will need to make the best of what stands around you now in the way of fun. You needn't take anything too seriously for the moment, and have scope to show the funniest and even the most ridiculous side of your nature.

29 SUNDAY *Moon Age Day 25 Moon Sign Taurus*

Even if today proves to be inspiring on a social level, the lunar low doesn't help you to finish what you start. For this reason you would be best advised to keep life light and steady. It would also be sensible to avoid too many risks and not to push yourself too hard in a physical sense. A day to slow the pace of life.

30 MONDAY
Moon Age Day 26   Moon Sign Taurus

Things may still be slower and less exciting than was the case last week, though this does at least give you the opportunity to look at matters more realistically and to deal with situations one at a time. Even if you are not exactly setting the world on fire, you can be more certain that your efforts will eventually bear fruit.

July

2008

1 TUESDAY
Moon Age Day 27 Moon Sign Gemini

The Sun, now in your solar ninth house, enhances your ability to concentrate and to get on well in a professional and practical way. At the same time other planetary trends bring a real yearning for some aspects of life to be the way they were in the past. Nostalgia is fine, but in the end you have to deal with the world the way it is.

2 WEDNESDAY
Moon Age Day 28 Moon Sign Gemini

There could be some hopeful and really interesting news coming in from far away. This is a good time for communicating with people at a distance, by whatever means you choose. Face-to-face communication is also important, especially with new friends and associates.

3 THURSDAY
Moon Age Day 0 Moon Sign Cancer

Career matters could be quite fulfilling, but there isn't much doubt that the most favoured part of your life at the moment will be associated with romance. If you have recently started a new relationship you should be able to put on a little pressure to intensify things, and Scorpio can really be the king or queen of love right now.

4 FRIDAY
Moon Age Day 1 Moon Sign Cancer

Today is good from a social point of view but probably less useful professionally. It doesn't matter how hard you try at the moment, it's difficult to get things to go the way you would wish in a practical sense. It would be better simply to go with the flow than to fight against the current of life so much.

5 SATURDAY
Moon Age Day 2 Moon Sign Leo

Charm and flattery can take you a long way today and you have exactly what it takes to make almost everyone you meet feel like the most important person in the world. Your capacity for love is off the scale and you can show your affection in so many different ways. Even people who didn't like you before may love you now!

6 SUNDAY
Moon Age Day 3 Moon Sign Leo

Now is a good time for co-operation and for getting together with like-minded individuals. This might not be possible professionally on a Sunday, but there are many other areas of life upon which you can concentrate. Now is the time to think about a new club or society, and to find incentives all around.

7 MONDAY
Moon Age Day 4 Moon Sign Virgo

There could be a few setbacks in practical matters, influenced by the present position of Mars in your solar chart. If you notice these at all they are likely to be very minor, because fiery Mars is usually a friend to Scorpio. Any new strategy or plan should be followed through with as much enthusiasm as you can muster.

8 TUESDAY
Moon Age Day 5 Moon Sign Virgo

Now you can afford to be taking a more prominent role, especially in situations that need a dose of sound, clear thinking. If people see you as being capable and practical in your approach, that stands you in good stead. What a good job they can't see how little genuine confidence you have on occasion. Scorpio is the master of disguise.

9 WEDNESDAY
Moon Age Day 6 Moon Sign Libra

You could discover today that self-determination is less of an option, particularly if you are more or less forced to follow the dictates of others. This is not a problem when you agree with them, but might cause you some aggravation when you know that you could do much better if you were only left to your own devices.

10 THURSDAY
Moon Age Day 7 Moon Sign Libra

Make the most of a potentially quieter spell as the Moon passes through your solar twelfth house. You can use today and tomorrow to catch up on things and to spend a little more time in the bosom of your family. The real gains come a little further down the line and for now, patience is your best response.

11 FRIDAY
Moon Age Day 8 Moon Sign Libra

No surprise if you are feeling slightly restless at the moment. The planetary line-up encourages you to feel like a car with the engine revving but the brakes firmly on. The best way round this is to put all that energy into planning what you intend to do once the race is really on. Lend a quiet hand to a friend who is having problems.

12 SATURDAY
Moon Age Day 9 Moon Sign Scorpio

Even if things do go slightly wrong today, you should find yourself in a good position to put them right almost instantly. Now there are few restrictions and your fertile mind can work overtime. The weekend as a whole has potential to be one of the best for a while and you need to react quickly to invitations and new possibilities.

13 SUNDAY
Moon Age Day 10 Moon Sign Scorpio

Just about anything you do today can be both interesting and productive, even if it doesn't necessarily seem that way. Your romance rating in the eyes of others is going off the scale, and you have what it takes to attract a good deal of attention from some fairly surprising directions.

14 MONDAY
Moon Age Day 11 Moon Sign Sagittarius

Today begins a period of fairly hectic comings and goings. With little time to catch your breath you are going to have to react quickly to changing circumstances and will be at your best if you can be in charge. What might be slightly lacking is your usual response to family members, which is now less positive than normal.

15 TUESDAY   *Moon Age Day 12   Moon Sign Sagittarius*

Your best approach, especially in discussions, is a much lighter touch and a warmth that might seem to be less obvious than usual. Take time out to make sure that others are aware of your concern because you can't take their attitudes for granted. It isn't so much a case of doing any more but rather making it plain how you feel.

16 WEDNESDAY   *Moon Age Day 13   Moon Sign Sagittarius*

Group encounters and places of entertainment could be high on your agenda today, even if you are not particularly looking for either. The potential for having good times and for attracting others to you is now much better, and you can positively spark when in the right sort of company. Use these trends to boost your popularity.

17 THURSDAY   *Moon Age Day 14   Moon Sign Capricorn*

Things should be easier in terms of your professional life, and if you are between jobs at the moment you should look more carefully than usual at any opportunities that come your way. Self-employed Scorpios may be the luckiest of all because this is a time when you should be able to gain new and more lucrative strings to your bow.

18 FRIDAY   *Moon Age Day 15   Moon Sign Capricorn*

Trifling matters and minor obligations might not mean very much to you, but they could keep you fairly busy today. The only frustration here is if they prevent you from doing exactly what you would wish – and this situation could continue for hours. When you finally do break free you can let others know how relieved you are.

19 SATURDAY   *Moon Age Day 16   Moon Sign Aquarius*

You can make this a positive and fruitful period romantically, but only if you take the time out to let your partner or sweetheart know just how important they are to you. When it comes to starting a new passion it's simply a case of being what you really are. Grandiose gestures are not necessary, but small tokens of your love might help.

20 SUNDAY
Moon Age Day 17 Moon Sign Aquarius

Help can be garnered from friends, and at very opportune moments. Don't assume you can do everything yourself, and seek both assistance and advice when you know in your heart that you are probably out of your depth. There are unlikely to be any strings attached, even when the help comes from colleagues or associates.

21 MONDAY
Moon Age Day 18 Moon Sign Aquarius

Even if some duties prove to be a real test of your patience at the start of this working week, your best response is to carry on as normal and to work through the dross. Later in the day you can be more captivated by the possibilities that life is throwing in your path, especially ones that really stretch you mentally.

22 TUESDAY
Moon Age Day 19 Moon Sign Pisces

Friends could well be extremely important to you right now and can help you to bring some real sunshine into your life. Speaking of sunshine, the summer is now really playing a part in your thinking, even if it is only at a subconscious level. The time is right to make the most of the good weather and long days.

23 WEDNESDAY
Moon Age Day 20 Moon Sign Pisces

If you really want to get on well in a financial and a practical way right now, it's worth tackling the grassroots issues of life. This might not be too interesting, but it is important to get the details right and is what leads to more dynamic successes further down the line. You can afford to stand up for someone who really needs your support.

24 THURSDAY
Moon Age Day 21 Moon Sign Aries

Casual contacts might not seem to be too important at the moment, but they may have a greater significance than seems to be the case. You can't afford to overlook details either, because these too could have a bearing on your life. The more you get things right first time now, the better should be the results in a week or two.

25 FRIDAY
Moon Age Day 22 Moon Sign Aries

This will be the last chance for a day or two to really show your mettle in practical ways. The lunar low ahead supports a quieter and less reactive interlude, though for today you still have what it takes to show your more positive side in public settings. When it comes to a particular social matter you needn't wait for an invitation.

26 SATURDAY
Moon Age Day 23 Moon Sign Taurus

This may not be the most dynamic weekend of the year by a long way, and for that you can thank the presence of the lunar low. However, this does not mean you need to be unhappy. As long as you accept that there are times when you need to rest and to recharge your batteries, today and tomorrow can be fine.

27 SUNDAY
Moon Age Day 24 Moon Sign Taurus

It's worth winding down any major activities, and many Scorpio people will presently be quite happy to find a comfortable spot in the sun and to sit and dream for a while. Some of the routine jobs that you usually undertake at the weekend might have to wait, because the lunar low does nothing to help your progress.

28 MONDAY
Moon Age Day 25 Moon Sign Gemini

Starting today you need to make life as varied and exciting as possible. This won't be especially hard if you dispel the effects of the lunar low very quickly. Be prepared to replace these with a greater sense of purpose and a determination to make your mark on life. Along the way you can impress others.

29 TUESDAY
Moon Age Day 26 Moon Sign Gemini

The present position of Venus in your solar chart assists you to move into the social mainstream and to make a good impression on many different sorts of people. You can afford to be chattier than normal, even if you are put on the spot. Love may also be found today.

30 WEDNESDAY   *Moon Age Day 27 Moon Sign Cancer*

Be on the lookout for new opportunities during the middle of this week and leave no stone unturned when it comes to seeking possibilities and adventures for the future. Scorpio people who have chosen this period to take a holiday could be some of the luckiest of all, and even short trips can offer scope for handsome rewards at the moment.

31 THURSDAY   *Moon Age Day 28 Moon Sign Cancer*

Certain major accomplishments remain possible, and it could seem as though some of the help you receive at the moment is divinely inspired. Being a Scorpio you are quite used to having to work hard for almost everything you get, but the planets are lending a significant hand at the moment. It's now up to you to do your bit.

August

2008

1 FRIDAY
Moon Age Day 0 Moon Sign Leo

The first day of August offers a chance to get busy with good ideas and the prospects life holds out for you. There might also be a busy schedule and some fairly heavy demands, but you can take these very much in your stride. Why not get in touch with friends or relatives at a distance and work out some way you can see them soon?

2 SATURDAY
Moon Age Day 1 Moon Sign Leo

It may not be exactly easy to get on with specific individuals today, especially those who seem to be awkward for no real reason. Nevertheless you would be wise to keep your cool and to be as charming and polite as possible. Not everyone seems to be working for your good at the moment, but you can ignore the odd misery.

3 SUNDAY
Moon Age Day 2 Moon Sign Virgo

Right now there are signs that you need friendship and affection in order to feel happy. That's why it can be just slightly distressing if someone seems to be ignoring you slightly. Rather than reacting too strongly, it might be worthwhile discovering whether something is bothering them. You might be able to help.

4 MONDAY
Moon Age Day 3 Moon Sign Virgo

You should particularly enjoy being out there in good company this week, and the show starts today. There are gains to be made by pushing yourself forward and by being willing to act as spokesperson for others. Even if people rely heavily on you today, you have what it takes to come through smiling.

5 TUESDAY
Moon Age Day 4 Moon Sign Virgo

Things could continue to be quite eventful, and you can harness a little more in the way of general good luck than might sometimes be the case. You can afford to back your hunches most of the time at present, but you also need to employ a good deal of common sense regarding relationship issues.

6 WEDNESDAY
Moon Age Day 5 Moon Sign Libra

You can ease things off somewhat for a couple of days ahead of the lunar high, and can use the time to think. Out here in the middle of the week you might be looking for answers that seem to elude you, and especially so at work. The best way forward is to enlist a degree of advice and also to draw on your past experience.

7 THURSDAY
Moon Age Day 6 Moon Sign Libra

Dealings with a wider social circle could mean having to put on a more public face, and that is something that may not be easy for the next twenty-four hours. Even if you would rather be on your own for most of the time, things have potential to change very rapidly tomorrow. In the meantime, you can at least appear to be interested.

8 FRIDAY
Moon Age Day 7 Moon Sign Scorpio

Help can be obtained from the most unlikely directions and at the most opportune times. Maybe it's simply that the lunar high gives you great opportunities to recognise assistance? Whatever you decide to do today should be tinged with a brilliance that helps you to win through, and to impress others on the way.

9 SATURDAY
Moon Age Day 8 Moon Sign Scorpio

If ever there was a good time during which to get others round to your way of thinking, this is it. You should also be at your very best and most attractive when it comes to knocking someone for six. The weekend offers a great deal to help you to feel better about yourself, and would be a fine time to be spreading your wings generally.

10 SUNDAY
Moon Age Day 9 Moon Sign Sagittarius

The emphasis is still on communication, and although the lunar high has now passed, you have potential to get on well in any situation that means standing up in public and talking the talk. You seem to be able to get through routines today with a smile on your face and a song on your lips.

11 MONDAY
Moon Age Day 10 Moon Sign Sagittarius

Your instincts should be well honed today, and you could do worse than to follow them under most circumstances. Look out for people who might be of use to you in a professional sense, but be careful about committing yourself without double-checking all the details. Rules could well get on your nerves.

12 TUESDAY
Moon Age Day 11 Moon Sign Sagittarius

Now is the time to use your diplomacy at home, perhaps to sort out some sort of disagreement or situation that has caused a rift. You can also play the honest broker at work, but it is important to remember that you must avoid taking sides in disputes. Rather, you need to stand aside and arbitrate.

13 WEDNESDAY
Moon Age Day 12 Moon Sign Capricorn

The present position of Venus in your solar chart suggests situations in personal relationships that seem custom-made to test your patience. Flying off the handle is not to be recommended. Instead, it might be better under most circumstances to count to ten first.

14 THURSDAY
Moon Age Day 13 Moon Sign Capricorn

Don't allow others to misunderstand you. It might be necessary to explain yourself more than once, and under all circumstances you need to be quite sure that those around you are in no doubt about your point of view. In matters of the heart you can show yourself to be a true romantic, and could gain brownie points as a result.

15 FRIDAY
Moon Age Day 14   Moon Sign Aquarius

There is still more enjoyment to be had now, with your love life being highlighted. There never was a better time to make someone aware of your feelings, and you have many ideas for underlining your affection. Things might be slightly more difficult with colleagues or associates, particularly any who are behaving a little oddly.

16 SATURDAY
Moon Age Day 15   Moon Sign Aquarius

If obstacles arise today, you need to proceed with a little more caution than you have been showing for the last few days. If it seems as though someone is trying to pull the wool over your eyes, this may indeed be the case. Your intuition is strong and is unlikely to let you down, which is why you can afford to rely on it so strongly now.

17 SUNDAY
Moon Age Day 16   Moon Sign Aquarius

You may decide to focus on particular objectives and concentrate on these, almost to the exclusion of everything else. That's fine as far as it goes but it does mean that on some occasions you could fail to see the wood for the trees. What is really needed is a more across-the-board attitude and great flexibility for most of the day.

18 MONDAY
Moon Age Day 17   Moon Sign Pisces

Trends suggest that career issues could be going slightly off course, and this is an ideal time to get the train back onto the track. Distractions are possible, some of which seem certain to throw you into a state of disarray, but the truth is that you have focus and staying power. It's simply a case of employing these.

19 TUESDAY
Moon Age Day 18   Moon Sign Pisces

Any attempt to be dominating in relationships is not helped by current influences. The more humble you appear, the greater is the chance that you can bring others round to your point of view. There is something very impulsive about Scorpio at the moment, which is fine just as long as you realise the fact and keep control.

20 WEDNESDAY *Moon Age Day 19 Moon Sign Aries*

Mars is now in your solar twelfth house, encouraging some agitation on your part. You will be less likely to get what you want from life if you constantly worry about things. The more matter-of-fact you seem to be when dealing with others, the greater is the chance that they will see your strengths and follow your ideas.

21 THURSDAY *Moon Age Day 20 Moon Sign Aries*

The past seems to have a great deal to do with your present thoughts, particularly if you are dwelling on issues from years ago that seem to have a bearing on the present. In reality you would be better off judging everything on its present merits and leaving nostalgia of any sort alone. Your attitude should be realistic and totally up-to-date.

22 FRIDAY *Moon Age Day 21 Moon Sign Taurus*

With the lunar low around you may not be at your luckiest, and you will need to be that much more discriminating in order to keep making progress. Actually you might decide to sit and take stock for a while, leaving others to do most of the hard work. In the meantime you can think up new strategies for next week.

23 SATURDAY *Moon Age Day 22 Moon Sign Taurus*

Although this might seem like a low point in your general fortunes, if you stop to analyse things fully you should see that you are actually doing rather well. Any problem at the moment exists more in your mind than it does in reality, and by tomorrow this will become obvious. For now your best option is to watch, wait and prepare.

24 SUNDAY *Moon Age Day 23 Moon Sign Gemini*

The focus is on security today. You need to know that others are rooting for you and that personal attachments are as sound as they can be. Once you have satisfied yourself you should be in a much better position to push forward positively and to enjoy fully what this August Sunday has to offer.

25 MONDAY *Moon Age Day 24 Moon Sign Gemini*

Trends now encourage you to be more independent and assertive than has been possible for quite a few days. Even if you feel as though the time is right to make a stand about something, it might be better if you waited just a little longer. Those same things that seem so important today will soon be getting less significant – even by tomorrow.

26 TUESDAY *Moon Age Day 25 Moon Sign Gemini*

This may not be the most enjoyable part of the month in terms of relationships, particularly if you don't feel able to knock people off their feet as well as you did a couple of weeks ago. Bear in mind that this might have little to do with your own capabilities, and everything to do with situations beyond your control.

27 WEDNESDAY *Moon Age Day 26 Moon Sign Cancer*

A day that emphasises a strong desire to help others and the charitable side of your nature. There's nothing especially odd about this because Scorpio gives half its life in service to others. What you offer in the way of assistance is practical and considered. Your specialist skills could be particularly welcome.

28 THURSDAY *Moon Age Day 27 Moon Sign Cancer*

You needn't be shy about your feelings today. Although it might not always be easy to do so, your best approach is to keep talking and to explain yourself fully. You can afford to become slightly more impulsive and to show less of a tendency to dig yourself into your own little hole. The Scorpion is beginning to emerge from its den.

29 FRIDAY *Moon Age Day 28 Moon Sign Leo*

It only takes a small amount of encouragement from others today for you to show what you are really made of. Instead of working all the time, why not put yourself in the market for some fun and enjoy yourself in the company of people you find to be approachable and good to be with.

30 SATURDAY

Moon Age Day 29   Moon Sign Leo

Mercury is in your solar twelfth house, doing little to enhance your ability to talk to specific individuals. Even if other people seem to be so much more eloquent than you think you are, you have the ability to match almost anyone, and only lack a little confidence in your own powers of communication.

31 SUNDAY

Moon Age Day 0   Moon Sign Virgo

Right now a strong need for reassurance is indicated, though only up to a point. As the day advances so you can afford to let your confidence grow and to rely less on the good offices of others. Any form of travel is well accented, and a late summer holiday would be ideal for most Scorpio people.

September

2008

1 MONDAY
Moon Age Day 1 Moon Sign Virgo

Scorpio now has scope to be much more innovative and to look repeatedly at new ways of getting on well, especially in a financial sense. Some things still come hard to you, but you can overcome obstacles fairly easily and show the world at large that you are equal to just about any task you choose to take on.

2 TUESDAY
Moon Age Day 2 Moon Sign Libra

As is often the case, the highly secretive side of your nature is highlighted and you will need to share your ideas and opinions more if you want to get others onside. This may not be especially easy for you, but your best approach is simply to curb your natural scepticism.

3 WEDNESDAY
Moon Age Day 3 Moon Sign Libra

Just like that feisty little creature for which your zodiac sign is named, you are inclined to hide in dark corners and to come out fighting at the first indication that someone is threatening you. This sort of behaviour is fine under some circumstances, but is certainly not necessary at the moment. A more open attitude still is called for.

4 THURSDAY
Moon Age Day 4 Moon Sign Scorpio

Now you can take the determination that is the hallmark of your sign and use it to the full. Even if you are far from being totally trusting of others, your ability to co-operate is getting better. Ally your skills with those of colleagues and friends and you can't go far wrong. Be prepared to get Lady Luck on your side.

5 FRIDAY
Moon Age Day 5 Moon Sign Scorpio

The potential for significant success is now strong, and all it really takes is an extra push from you to make almost everything go your way. Actually nothing is really very different than it has been for days. It's simply your state of mind that has changed, and in the end that can make all the difference in the world.

6 SATURDAY
Moon Age Day 6 Moon Sign Scorpio

You can continue to bask in the positive light of the lunar high and should be starting the weekend feeling optimistic and quite certain of your own powers and abilities. Now is the time to get together with like-minded individuals and find new ways to have fun. At the same time you can show your charitable side more strongly than ever.

7 SUNDAY
Moon Age Day 7 Moon Sign Sagittarius

Being naturally courageous you may be more willing than your friends to do something that is just slightly dangerous. That's fine just as long as the risks you take are calculated. What you don't need today is to put yourself in peril for no good reason. In all probability the person you most want to impress at the moment is yourself!

8 MONDAY
Moon Age Day 8 Moon Sign Sagittarius

You might now decide to spend more time on your own, mainly because you need space to think and can't do so when there are people constantly chatting in your ear. These periods of withdrawal are nothing unusual for Scorpio and are part of the way you keep your head straight. Money matters look settled.

9 TUESDAY
Moon Age Day 9 Moon Sign Capricorn

Influences change once again as the Moon in particular moves on, offering a more sociable period and a time during which you can make gains by being in the right place at the most opportune time. Your love life can be given a more romantic feel, particularly if you are putting in a little more effort now.

10 WEDNESDAY *Moon Age Day 10 Moon Sign Capricorn*

The domestic scene is one of your best areas at the moment, but it is far from being the only one. Friends could well make demands on your time and your experience. Even if you have little time to call your own, by making the most of favourable trends you can show a contented and happy face to the world.

11 THURSDAY *Moon Age Day 11 Moon Sign Capricorn*

Don't expect to get all your own way when it comes to your love life just at the moment. If you really want to make your partner or sweetheart happy you might have to make significant concessions, even to the point of burying your own wishes for a while. However, the results should make the inconvenience more than worthwhile.

12 FRIDAY *Moon Age Day 12 Moon Sign Aquarius*

As you push ahead with various plans at the moment it's worth looking out for any problems. You will need to keep your wits about you and it will be necessary to react quickly in order to keep things on track. The situation may be worse if you are constantly having to do the same job more than once.

13 SATURDAY *Moon Age Day 13 Moon Sign Aquarius*

A number of enjoyable moments are possible this weekend, though with Venus in your solar twelfth house you may not be going through the very best period of your life in a personal sense. Rather than remaining locked inside yourself emotionally, why not try to express your innermost feelings?

14 SUNDAY *Moon Age Day 14 Moon Sign Pisces*

Mars is also in your solar twelfth house, which again encourages withdrawal, and maybe a little frustration if you can't say what you really want. It's worth remaining tactful, because the most difficult situations for Scorpio come along when you speak without thinking and upset the applecart as a result.

15 MONDAY
Moon Age Day 15 Moon Sign Pisces

You clearly have scope to get ahead at the start of this week, especially in a practical sense, but there are situations that need constant checking and verification. This might slow you down somewhat and make certain aspects of life a little tedious. What you need is something different to do once the demands of work are out of the way.

16 TUESDAY
Moon Age Day 16 Moon Sign Aries

It looks as though some of the practicalities of life could get a little easier today. However, your magnetic side is not to the fore. All of those twelfth-house planetary influences encourage you to turn in on yourself but fortunately this is not a situation that lasts for long. Be patient, because things are changing.

17 WEDNESDAY
Moon Age Day 17 Moon Sign Aries

In all probability you long to change things significantly – by travel if necessary. This is possible but rather less than likely, particularly if there is too much else to do. Perhaps you are overstressing your own importance to certain situations. It's time to delegate and to allow others to take on some more of the responsibility.

18 THURSDAY
Moon Age Day 18 Moon Sign Aries

You can afford to speak your mind today, even if what you have to say isn't very popular with everyone. In the end you can only succeed if you are truthful to yourself, and you won't manage that if you worry too much about the sensibilities of everyone else. You can be of great help to family members and friends who have problems.

19 FRIDAY
Moon Age Day 19 Moon Sign Taurus

The lunar low suggests you should be patient and allow things to mature in their own good time. What you can't afford to do today or tomorrow is to push issues too hard. For one thing you might soon run out of energy and could find things crowding in on you when you least expect it. At least you can keep finances fairly settled.

20 SATURDAY
Moon Age Day 20 Moon Sign Taurus

If your personal influence regarding everyday issues is somewhat diminished, this alone could lead to further frustrations. The best way round the potential problems is to maintain your sense of humour and to show just how resilient you can be. There are always alternatives, and a little adversity allows you to find them.

21 SUNDAY
Moon Age Day 21 Moon Sign Gemini

Along with a host of other planets, little Mercury occupies your solar twelfth house, which supports a less chatty approach in which you are more inclined to stick to your own inner feelings. There is no doubt that Scorpio is going through a prolonged insular period, but once planetary circumstances change the feeling of freedom is going to be fantastic!

22 MONDAY
Moon Age Day 22 Moon Sign Gemini

Career success can now be achieved through a combination of originality and your present ability to think deeply. Although co-operation is favoured today, you may still choose to do most things yourself and avoid getting involved in the schemes and machinations of others.

23 TUESDAY
Moon Age Day 23 Moon Sign Cancer

You have what it takes to be fascinating to others – if only because they find it impossible to know what makes you tick. Keep up this air of mystery because it can be of assistance to you at the moment. Money matters should be more settled and you could be drawing on resources that you didn't expect to have.

24 WEDNESDAY
Moon Age Day 24 Moon Sign Cancer

The accent now is on close, personal relationships much more than it will be on more casual attachments. Be wary of trying out new situations and possibilities, at least not until you are very sure that the basis of your life is solid. Scorpio may not be at its must humorous at the moment, but you can make sure you have your moments.

25 THURSDAY ☿ *Moon Age Day 25 Moon Sign Leo*

·You have scope to seek out more warmth today, assisted by the shifting position of the Moon. Despite a potential lack of self-confidence it is possible that colleagues and friends will rely on you quite heavily. Trends enhance your ability to attract compliments, and you need to believe them.

26 FRIDAY ☿ *Moon Age Day 26 Moon Sign Leo*

Getting out and about does increase your chance of learning things that are going to be of significance to you in a general sense, and it also broadens your horizons at a time when you may be quite insular. The only difficulty is forcing yourself to do things that your inner mind tells you are going to be hard and maybe a waste of effort.

27 SATURDAY ☿ *Moon Age Day 27 Moon Sign Virgo*

Even if your quiet side is to the fore at the moment you remain, in your heart at least, the same old warrior that Scorpio generally is. You won't tolerate seeing anyone mistreated and your charitable nature is turned up full across this particular weekend. You can also establish more positive relationships at home.

28 SUNDAY ☿ *Moon Age Day 28 Moon Sign Virgo*

It may not seem that you are really at your best in social situations but others find you fun to be around and you can exploit your present sardonic sense of humour to the full. The results are that you can have a good time, almost despite yourself, and that you can continue to impress people even when there is no real reason to do so.

29 MONDAY ☿ *Moon Age Day 29 Moon Sign Libra*

A twelfth-house Moon at the start of this week emphasises your present need to go it alone for most of the time, and it may occur to you that September has not been the most positive month of the year so far. However, to really see what you have achieved in the present period it will be necessary to view it from a distance – so keep trucking!

30 TUESDAY ☿ *Moon Age Day 0 Moon Sign Libra*

Comfort can be found in routines, and you would be wise to avoid taking undue chances just for the moment. The real strong point this week comes from Thursday on, and in the meantime you can best prepare yourself by getting existing jobs out of the way. You have the potential to work long and hard right now.

October 2008

1 WEDNESDAY ☿ *Moon Age Day 1 Moon Sign Libra*

There could be slight monetary gains on offer, some assisted by simple good luck. At the same time you can be fairly sure that your ability to discriminate will be very good and you needn't take unnecessary chances with cash. Sort out social priorities today because things could get a whole lot busier from tomorrow.

2 THURSDAY ☿ *Moon Age Day 2 Moon Sign Scorpio*

Now you have scope to look and feel at your best. The Moon is in Scorpio and all those twelfth-house planets are getting closer and closer to your solar first house. A professional plan of action could well turn out far luckier than you might have expected, but in the main this is thanks to your own hard work and far-sightedness.

3 FRIDAY ☿ *Moon Age Day 3 Moon Sign Scorpio*

Today marks a physical and mental peak and rehearses some of the better planetary trends that will be around you during much of October. Your judgement is especially well accented, and you can see through other people just as surely as if they were made of glass. This allows you a greater ability to predict what reactions to expect.

4 SATURDAY ☿ *Moon Age Day 4 Moon Sign Sagittarius*

The time is gradually coming right for you to take centre stage, and even if you are still just a little reticent to push yourself forward, you can seek reassurance from others. Some of that famous Scorpio magnetism is now on display and best of all you should actually 'feel' as though the tide is turning in your favour.

5 SUNDAY
☿ *Moon Age Day 5 Moon Sign Sagittarius*

Although there is unlikely to be enough time available today to do everything you might wish, you are still like a child in a sweet shop when it comes to the possibilities that surround you. Little by little you should be growing and stretching – fitting your nature for the potential that is on offer across the next couple of weeks.

6 MONDAY
☿ *Moon Age Day 6 Moon Sign Sagittarius*

Today's trends encourage you to see things in terms of the way they will have a bearing on your personal and family life. The world beyond your own door is not quite as important as might sometimes be the case, and you can become a slightly more private sort of person. This is not at all unusual for Scorpio from time to time.

7 TUESDAY
☿ *Moon Age Day 7 Moon Sign Capricorn*

Be prepared to keep an eye on fluctuating finances. Maybe you have been a little too lavish of late, though you can get cash reserves looking better again before the end of this month. An ideal day for local news and improvements to the area where you live.

8 WEDNESDAY
☿ *Moon Age Day 8 Moon Sign Capricorn*

The focus is still on finance, offering you scope to find ways to improve things, even if the plans you put into action today won't mature for a week or two. At the same time trends encourage you to be slightly more outgoing and to respond positively to things that will draw you out of your own little corner.

9 THURSDAY
☿ *Moon Age Day 9 Moon Sign Aquarius*

If you want to be really happy at the moment you need to be creative and to join in with all the fun and games that is on offer. Some Scorpios presently may be taking a slightly gloomy view of the way life is going, and it is important that you don't allow yourself to be one of them. Keep busy, stay well and laugh a lot!

10 FRIDAY   ☿ *Moon Age Day 10 Moon Sign Aquarius*

As the month wears on you can afford to let your ego grow stronger and to develop better and better ways to make people take notice of you. This process begins now as several planets edge themselves towards your solar first house. People might not be hanging on your every word, but you can at least get them to look your way.

11 SATURDAY   ☿ *Moon Age Day 11 Moon Sign Aquarius*

Venus is now in your solar first house and that offers a definite boost to relationships. The way you view yourself often has much to do with the affection that you can gain from others. Since you are gradually becoming flavour of the month, you should also begin to get much more confident – a process that starts right now.

12 SUNDAY   ☿ *Moon Age Day 12 Moon Sign Pisces*

If you keep well organised, you shouldn't go far wrong. Although there is no particular rush about life just at the moment you should recognise that it would be best to grab opportunities whilst they are around. Friends could be equally busy, and might not always be able to drop everything just to suit your particular needs.

13 MONDAY   ☿ *Moon Age Day 13 Moon Sign Pisces*

You would be wise to avoid confrontation because you really don't need any arguments in your life just now. Being friends with everyone might prove to be difficult but is certainly not impossible. They say it takes two to tango, and if you don't want to fall out with anyone, no situation will change your mind.

14 TUESDAY   ☿ *Moon Age Day 14 Moon Sign Aries*

It's time to be broadening your personal horizons. It's a fact about autumn-born Scorpio that when everyone else is starting to slow down for the winter, you are just getting into gear. The thought of shorter days and colder weather does little or nothing to dent your enthusiasm, and you can afford to be especially optimistic today.

15 WEDNESDAY ☿ *Moon Age Day 15 Moon Sign Aries*

The forces of change are now well in place and you should be looking out towards a horizon that is a good deal more settled and potentially prosperous than anything you have recognised for the last month or so. There are going to be a couple of less positive days to come but these are only a minor setback and shouldn't be taken too seriously.

16 THURSDAY ☿ *Moon Age Day 16 Moon Sign Taurus*

Put major issues on the back burner and do what you can to consolidate your position today. The lunar low doesn't bring positive trends but at the same time you need to realise that you can move forward, even if it seems a slow journey for the moment. An ideal time to seek affection from friends and relatives.

17 FRIDAY *Moon Age Day 17 Moon Sign Taurus*

Now you really do need to take things one at a time, particularly if you have a temporary inability to hold as much in your mind as would normally be the case. One job done properly is worth ten that you have to address again later, but remember that you can change things significantly tomorrow.

18 SATURDAY *Moon Age Day 18 Moon Sign Gemini*

Keep your eyes open today because there are new opportunities on offer, all of which seem custom-designed for you to bring more fun into your life. You can now show a far greater sense of resilience and a determination to break down barriers if necessary in order to get where you want to be. Romance is especially well starred at present.

19 SUNDAY *Moon Age Day 19 Moon Sign Gemini*

In three or four days' time the Sun will move into your solar first house, but it has been beaten to that spot by Venus, which is already helping you to light up your life in a romantic sense. It also encourages you to be more refined and to shun anything you see as being shabby or lacking in finesse. Your appearance becomes very important now.

20 MONDAY
Moon Age Day 20 Moon Sign Cancer

What you really manage to do at the moment is to get the very best out of almost everyone you come across. Part of this is down to astrological influences but it can be aided by your own attitude, which should now be much more positive and determined. Why not make contact with someone who lives at a distance?

21 TUESDAY
Moon Age Day 21 Moon Sign Cancer

Financial security means a lot to you and could be especially important just at the moment. You have scope to look ahead and seek ways to be better off for the future, and to dream up ideas that will make you more comfortable at home. Don't get too carried away though, because there are some changes in store that are necessary.

22 WEDNESDAY
Moon Age Day 22 Moon Sign Leo

An ideal day to get out there and make new friends. It is very important at the moment to make the best of impressions on just about anyone, and this could be especially important at work. Even if mixing business with pleasure isn't something you do much as a rule, it can stand you in good stead under present planetary trends.

23 THURSDAY
Moon Age Day 23 Moon Sign Leo

There is a great deal of interesting information around right now, and you absorb so much on your daily journey through life that it all takes a great deal of synthesising. That doesn't matter because you can put what you gather on a shelf in your brain and analyse it later. What matters is simply learning more and more.

24 FRIDAY
Moon Age Day 24 Moon Sign Virgo

Today the Sun enters your solar first house and brings with it that part of the year during which you have a chance to make significant gains and to be at your best in most situations. You can afford to be feeling far more confident than you were a couple of weeks ago, and part of this has to do with your ability to work through sticky patches.

25 SATURDAY
Moon Age Day 25 Moon Sign Virgo

Even if you aren't taking anything for granted at the moment, you can afford to be slightly blasé about irrelevant details. From a social point of view you enjoy yourself most this weekend if you simply respond to offers that are coming in, and much of what really makes you happy right now is totally spontaneous.

26 SUNDAY
Moon Age Day 26 Moon Sign Virgo

You might sense that in some ways a more frugal approach is necessary, and if so it's worth drawing your horns in from a financial point of view. It is possible that this attitude has something to do with the fact that you realise Christmas is not that far away, or it may simply be that you have a project in mind that will require money.

27 MONDAY
Moon Age Day 27 Moon Sign Libra

Opportunities for greater success are available, though there may be times when you will have to pay attention if you are not to be beaten to the punch by someone else! Keep your wits about you and avoid hesitation. The motto of the SAS is 'Who dares wins', and this is especially appropriate to Scorpio at the moment.

28 TUESDAY
Moon Age Day 28 Moon Sign Libra

Even if you continue to be progressive and determined, this might not get you exactly what you want today. With a twelfth-house Moon there could be delays and you may also notice that loved ones are not exactly helpful or co-operative. By tomorrow everything will look different and your efforts will not be going to waste.

29 WEDNESDAY
Moon Age Day 0 Moon Sign Scorpio

A high-energy point comes along and you shouldn't waste a single moment of what can be the most progressive period of the month. Get up early and sort yourself out as quickly as possible. If you follow your intuition you can make the most of the luck that is on offer. Any risks you take at the moment are extremely calculated.

30 THURSDAY
Moon Age Day 1 Moon Sign Scorpio

The lunar high is an extremely good time to be putting new ideas to the test and for persuading others to help you as a matter of course. Your attitude can be so positive that it is difficult to see how anyone could fail to recognise your potential. Most important of all your happy nature and bright, smiling face are all you need to captivate the world.

31 FRIDAY
Moon Age Day 2 Moon Sign Sagittarius

If you look and feel strong, others will probably take it for granted that you can achieve almost anything. There is no point in telling them that this is not the case, so you may as well believe it yourself. Rather than getting tied down today with pointless routines, be prepared to take gains where you find them and push for what you really want.

November

2008

1 SATURDAY
Moon Age Day 3   Moon Sign Sagittarius

The emphasis at the very start of November is on resourcefulness and your natural ability to look after personal finances. Scorpio can be extremely shrewd and never more so than under present trends. Your ability to look ahead and to make the right decisions now can be almost uncanny. Why not get friends to follow your lead?

2 SUNDAY
Moon Age Day 4   Moon Sign Sagittarius

Give and take is important at home, especially if certain family members are behaving in a less than typical way. Fortunately this needn't be the case in a romantic sense. In this area of your life you know exactly what to say and will also have a good idea about what makes your partner tick. A timely gift can make all the difference.

3 MONDAY
Moon Age Day 5   Moon Sign Capricorn

Beware of getting too carried away today because even if life looks exciting you also need to focus on what is really important. Any distractions could cause you to miss some positive opportunities, particularly financial ones. All it really takes is for you to keep your eyes and ears open.

4 TUESDAY
Moon Age Day 6   Moon Sign Capricorn

You seem to have considerable charm at your disposal now and should be quite comfortable in situations that put you in the spotlight. This isn't always the case for Scorpio, but for the moment you can make sure the shy side of your nature is taking a holiday. It's worth giving some attention to progress at work while the Sun is in your first house.

5 WEDNESDAY
Moon Age Day 7 Moon Sign Aquarius

Today offers scope to have fun and to involve as many people as you can in some of your ingenious schemes. Not all of these are going to work out quite the way you might have intended, but even if you only succeed in ten percent you should end November somewhat better off than you began it.

6 THURSDAY
Moon Age Day 8 Moon Sign Aquarius

Your powers of concentration are well accented, and will continue to be so throughout much of November. This assists you to plan long term and there is also a good chance that some of your efforts from earlier in the year are now starting to bear fruit. It might be necessary today to show that you can be very persuasive.

7 FRIDAY
Moon Age Day 9 Moon Sign Aquarius

Trends encourage a need to feel useful today, and you might be doing all you can to be supportive of both colleagues and friends. Once the routine aspects of the day are dealt with, the time will be right to have some fun. Involve family members if you can, but it is especially important to make sure your partner plays a part in things.

8 SATURDAY
Moon Age Day 10 Moon Sign Pisces

Mars is now in your solar first house, which is about as good as it gets for Scorpio because the Sun is there too. You can afford to be more dynamic and driving than has been the case throughout the whole year. If you can't get what you want from life right now, it's worth asking yourself whether you are trying as hard as you should.

9 SUNDAY
Moon Age Day 11 Moon Sign Pisces

The time seems right to tighten up certain securities, which ought to help you to feel more comfortable with your life in a general sense. Not everyone might have your best interests at heart right now. Your best approach is to show yourself to be shrewd and attentive, which reduces the chances of anyone duping you.

10 MONDAY
Moon Age Day 12 Moon Sign Aries

The trends are good financially, even if you have to put in some extra effort to get things moving in exactly the way you would wish. It is very important right now to feel that you are in charge of your own destiny because you won't work half as well if you feel that you are being constrained by the expectations of others.

11 TUESDAY
Moon Age Day 13 Moon Sign Aries

There isn't much doubt about your ability to get on extremely well with those people you care about the most, but what might be even more important is your response to virtual strangers. The usual Scorpio suspicion can be put to one side, assisting you to make new friends at every turn. These could prove to be significant.

12 WEDNESDAY
Moon Age Day 14 Moon Sign Taurus

If you show any problem during the lunar low this month it will be a tendency to worry too much about details. For most Scorpios the positive planetary trends are so good that the lunar low will pass virtually unnoticed. Now would be a good time to get on with those last-minute changes around the house ahead of the winter.

13 THURSDAY
Moon Age Day 15 Moon Sign Taurus

You would be wise to leave any major decisions until tomorrow, unless of course you have no choice. In situations where you can't delay you could do worse than to enlist the support and advice of a family member or a particularly good friend. Specialised jobs should be left to experts for the moment, or you could end up costing yourself money.

14 FRIDAY
Moon Age Day 16 Moon Sign Gemini

You have what it takes to show yourself in a new light, particularly to people who haven't noticed you at all so far this year. Energy levels are enhanced, assisting you to revel in any opportunity to get involved socially. Even if you are extremely busy, you can still find sufficient time to do almost everything you wish.

15 SATURDAY
Moon Age Day 17 Moon Sign Gemini

The present position of the Moon, taken together with all those first-house planets, is widening your mental horizons and leading you to possibilities you might not have thought of before. Don't take anything for granted and pay attention to the details of life. You now have what it takes to prove yourself in ways that will surprise even you.

16 SUNDAY
Moon Age Day 18 Moon Sign Cancer

What you seem to be striving for today is a peaceful and contented home life. Whilst this is yours for the taking it is unlikely to be the end of the story, because as soon as you sit down in your favourite chair you may well become restless and want to be on the move again. It could seem as if you have ants in your pants!

17 MONDAY
Moon Age Day 19 Moon Sign Cancer

Both home and career offer their own particular kind of rewards. A journey into the past may be necessary in order to sort something out that lies ahead of you, though in this case there is no troublesome nostalgia. You can use it to make sure that previous mistakes will not be repeated. Romance looms large in your life now.

18 TUESDAY
Moon Age Day 20 Moon Sign Leo

If you want to make sure that everything you say is clearly understood you might have to make your position extremely clear. Don't worry that others will tire of hearing your voice. On the contrary, you have what it takes to be just about as popular as it is possible to be, whilst at the same time getting what you want from life.

19 WEDNESDAY
Moon Age Day 21 Moon Sign Leo

Trends enhance your ability to organise things this week, to put yourself in the driving seat and to persuade others to follow your lead. Confidence remains high but there could be occasions when the weight of so much responsibility is heavy on your shoulders. If so, you can afford to share some of it.

20 THURSDAY   *Moon Age Day 22   Moon Sign Leo*

Once again if business or practical issues are up for discussion you have potential to take a leading role. You seem to have some really good ideas at the moment and should be quite happy to throw these in for what they are worth. Not an ideal day for progress in matters of love, so some patience would be wise.

21 FRIDAY   *Moon Age Day 23   Moon Sign Virgo*

This can be a hardworking period, to such an extent that you might overtax yourself if you are not careful. Despite all the positive trends that surround you, even Scorpio is only human. The best of all situations would be one in which you could begin your weekend a day early. Try to do something that isn't important but is enjoyable.

22 SATURDAY   *Moon Age Day 24   Moon Sign Virgo*

With the focus on enjoyment, you may not be thinking about progress of any sort. The one exception might be a desire to do well in sporting activities. Scorpio hates to be beaten and this facet of your nature is more strongly emphasised now than would normally be the case. Use it to your advantage.

23 SUNDAY   *Moon Age Day 25   Moon Sign Libra*

A day to turn your mind towards pleasing your nearest and dearest, but without pushing yourself beyond your own limits. The Moon is in your solar twelfth house and this supports a sluggish interlude when you are less inclined to be putting yourself at the front of any queue. Rules could really get on your nerves, so avoid them.

24 MONDAY   *Moon Age Day 26   Moon Sign Libra*

Today is good for getting ready and less positive when it comes to actions. The more you arrange and rearrange things, the greater should be your progress from tomorrow, by which time the Moon will be in your own zodiac sign. A little subterfuge might be necessary if you want to help someone who is reluctant to take your advice.

25 TUESDAY
Moon Age Day 27 Moon Sign Scorpio

Right now you should find both your personal and practical aims to be more than achievable. You should be realistic in your expectations and avoid doing anything that threatens your position in life either now or for the future. When it comes to the pleasure side of your life, you should be more than willing to push your luck a little.

26 WEDNESDAY
Moon Age Day 28 Moon Sign Scorpio

Once again if business initiatives need attention you should be right in your element. A slight change comes along with regard to romance. If you have been somewhat reticent to speak your true feelings for the last few days, trends now encourage you to spill out the truth. This turns out to be a good thing.

27 THURSDAY
Moon Age Day 29 Moon Sign Scorpio

You can use what you hear from others today to contribute to the current progressive phase. The only slight fly in the ointment comes from colleagues or friends who promise more than they deliver. Keep on top of situations, and if you can't rely on others, get cracking yourself. Energy remains well starred.

28 FRIDAY
Moon Age Day 0 Moon Sign Sagittarius

There is just a slight risk that you are putting your point of view rather too forcefully at the moment, and it might be good to allow others more time on the platform. This is not something that can be seen as a fault because as a rule you are more than ready to be democratic. It occurs simply because you are so keen to keep up the momentum.

29 SATURDAY
Moon Age Day 1 Moon Sign Sagittarius

If you try to achieve too much, you might find certain projects grinding to a halt. Your best response is to drop half of your expectations for the moment and concentrate on issues that are very nearly sorted. That way you will also have time to have fun, which is probably more important than anything at this stage of November.

30 SUNDAY
Moon Age Day 2 Moon Sign Capricorn

You can make sure things are working well for you as this most fortunate month draws to a close. The realisation that December is about to start could come as something of a shock, particularly if you have been too busy to look at the calendar. Why not spend some time today listening carefully to the opinions of others?

December

2008

1 MONDAY
Moon Age Day 3   Moon Sign Capricorn

The focus is on strong domestic ties at the beginning of December. It could be that your adventures in the outside world are somewhat curtailed as a result of home-based needs. On the other hand, there are so many planetary trends linking you to home and family at the moment that you may be entirely happy with your lot.

2 TUESDAY
Moon Age Day 4   Moon Sign Capricorn

There isn't much doubt that you can now be the life and soul of the party and that others instinctively show a fondness for you. Since your popularity is now so high you might as well use it to your advantage in order to get what you need. In most cases it could be a simple matter of asking in the right way.

3 WEDNESDAY
Moon Age Day 5   Moon Sign Aquarius

You have potential to be fairly progressive at the moment and to shake others out of their lethargy. The only difficulty could come if you have to confront individuals who seem more certain of themselves than you are. It could be the clash of the titans, particularly if you allow your stubborn side to prevail.

4 THURSDAY
Moon Age Day 6   Moon Sign Aquarius

Along comes a period when hard work is favoured – not that this is much of a problem to Scorpio at the present time. For weeks now you have been putting in so much effort that you must be near to achieving some significant results. If that seems rather unlikely today, this might be because your perspectives are temporarily clouded.

5 FRIDAY
Moon Age Day 7 Moon Sign Pisces

Venus is now in your solar third house, encouraging you to verbalise the affection you feel. You might even become a poet under present trends and certainly have what it takes to sweep people completely off their feet. This is just as relevant if your primary relationship is already years old.

6 SATURDAY
Moon Age Day 8 Moon Sign Pisces

Travel and conversations are both positively highlighted now, and although Christmas is still some weeks away you might already be getting yourself into the right frame of mind. Any sort of invitation seems ideal and you have what it takes to cheer up individuals who are not generally known for their happy attitude.

7 SUNDAY
Moon Age Day 9 Moon Sign Pisces

For some Scorpio people it could now seem as if everyone else is getting ahead faster. Today's trends support this frustration, particularly in terms of family ties or strained relationships generally. This can spill over into other areas of your life – most of all for weekend-working Scorpios.

8 MONDAY
Moon Age Day 10 Moon Sign Aries

Mental effort intensifies now, and although you will have the lunar low to contend with later this week, in the meantime you can push ahead very progressively. You needn't worry too much about missed opportunities because there are so many possibilities facing you at present that you cannot utilise them all.

9 TUESDAY
Moon Age Day 11 Moon Sign Aries

Today offers scope for you to make quick decisions, but this could well upset others. This is especially true if you are faced with people who seem to be deliberately getting things wrong. More patience is required, plus a better understanding of human nature.

10 WEDNESDAY   *Moon Age Day 12 Moon Sign Taurus*

Mental effort is not assisted by the Moon in Taurus. Clouded judgements and a degree of pessimism could be the result. Realising that the lunar low is a temporary thing, you ought to be able to take slight reversals in your stride, whilst at the same time slowing down somewhat.

11 THURSDAY   *Moon Age Day 13 Moon Sign Taurus*

If your energies are flagging it will be important to slow things down and to avoid making decisions unless you know you have thought any matter through carefully. By tomorrow this slight cloud on the horizon of your life should have disappeared, and you have everything you need to get back to your former positive ways.

12 FRIDAY   *Moon Age Day 14 Moon Sign Gemini*

What matters most about life just now is your burning sense of independence and your desire to break down barriers that may have stood for quite some time. At work you can make the best impression of all, and can prove yourself time and again. There may still be a few personal frustrations to be dealt with.

13 SATURDAY   *Moon Age Day 15 Moon Sign Gemini*

There isn't much doubt about your wit and sense of humour, both of which are on offer in great measure. Now is the time to use them in your dealings with others. Whether you can keep up with everything your social life puts in front of you is a different matter. You are, after all, only one person.

14 SUNDAY   *Moon Age Day 16 Moon Sign Cancer*

Try to slow things down a little, not because you lack either energy or incentive but simply because you need to enjoy what life gives you freely at present. It isn't so long until Christmas comes along, and many Scorpios are already in a festive spirit. New opportunities come thick and fast, but some may be ultimately delayed.

15 MONDAY
Moon Age Day 17 Moon Sign Cancer

Venus in your solar fourth house is going to be a great incentive to look carefully at what is happening in and around your home. It isn't unusual for Scorpio to become quite nostalgic and very warm towards family ties at this time of year. As a result, you may decide not to burn the social candle at the start of this week.

16 TUESDAY
Moon Age Day 18 Moon Sign Leo

Friendships can continue to be a source of joy and contentment and you also have what it takes to turn a casual attachment into something much deeper. Don't get too tied down today with rules or instructions because you will get by much better if you interpret things fairly liberally. Be prepared to deal with frustrations at work.

17 WEDNESDAY
Moon Age Day 19 Moon Sign Leo

Mental organisation and efficiency is not all it might be today, mainly because of the position of the Moon. This does not mean you can't achieve anything, merely that you will have to be fairly selective in what you take on. Social trends are better, offering you scope to entertain and to enjoy festive functions.

18 THURSDAY
Moon Age Day 20 Moon Sign Virgo

It isn't so much the concrete gains that you can achieve today that make you feel good. Rather, you have what it takes to enjoy the cut and thrust of all sorts of relationships and to be about as warm and charming as Scorpio is capable of being. Don't be afraid to attract attention.

19 FRIDAY
Moon Age Day 21 Moon Sign Virgo

You needn't restrict yourself to a strictly orthodox approach in discussions and might even argue against your own best interests on occasion today. Sticking to what you believe to be true, you can't go far wrong, even though it might look as though you are shooting yourself in the foot. At the moment your principles are important.

20 SATURDAY
Moon Age Day 22 Moon Sign Libra

Even if you remain socially and romantically active and attractive, trends assist you to shower most of your love and affection on family members. You approach Christmas with Venus in your solar fourth house, a part of the zodiac that deals specifically with domestic matters. Younger people especially can bask in the warmth you create.

21 SUNDAY
Moon Age Day 23 Moon Sign Libra

Don't be afraid to take the credit for some fairly bold ideas, even if from your point of perspective you are simply doing what seems most logical. It might be slightly difficult to deal with some of the compliments that are coming your way in a more general sense because you don't deal all that well with praise.

22 MONDAY
Moon Age Day 24 Moon Sign Scorpio

At least the lunar high for December comes at a time when you really need a physical and mental boost – in that final run-up to Christmas. Make full use of your energy to dash about from pillar to post, sorting out those last details. There should still be plenty of time for having fun, especially in the company of valued friends.

23 TUESDAY
Moon Age Day 25 Moon Sign Scorpio

Physical and mental strength remains an important factor and you can embark on new projects, even so close to Christmas, with absolute belief in your own abilities. Much of your present ability to get things done is turned towards your home surroundings, where you can get everything in place for an almost idyllic holiday period.

24 WEDNESDAY
Moon Age Day 26 Moon Sign Scorpio

For the third day in a row the Moon occupies your own zodiac sign of Scorpio, bringing you a sense of purpose and a determination that is greater than that felt by almost any other zodiac sign. If there is one thing you need to avoid today it is getting too bogged down with specific details. A broad overview of life works best.

25 THURSDAY   *Moon Age Day 27 Moon Sign Sagittarius*

Christmas Day ought to work out very well for you, though the best trends come when you are at home, amongst those you love the most. If you have to travel you may find that there are delays or slight difficulties, though your present nature is such that very little should hold you up for more than a few minutes.

26 FRIDAY   *Moon Age Day 28 Moon Sign Sagittarius*

This is a time of stimulating possibilities and especially so as far as your love life is concerned. Younger or unattached Scorpio people can capitalise on new love opportunities and romance is definitely to the fore. You have what it takes to make Christmas quite enchanting this time around.

27 SATURDAY   *Moon Age Day 0 Moon Sign Capricorn*

There are trends around right now that help you to sharpen your mental faculties and come up with new ideas. Originality is now the key to the greatest success, even if you get slightly frustrated because you can't make things happen as quickly as you would wish. You may already be tiring of Christmas excess!

28 SUNDAY   *Moon Age Day 1 Moon Sign Capricorn*

Trends support a slightly over-emotional tendency today. This is partly due to the position of the Moon but could also be a response to the time of year. Try to stay cool and steady in your approach to family matters, and if possible spend at least part of today in the company of friends, whose needs of you are quite different.

29 MONDAY   *Moon Age Day 2 Moon Sign Capricorn*

Life remains potentially rewarding, even if you do start to become slightly restless. If this is the case you may have to think up something to make you feel more needed and useful. It could seem as though you are standing on the sidelines, whilst others are making all the decisions but in reality you can be more in charge than you think.

30 TUESDAY   *Moon Age Day 3   Moon Sign Aquarius*

Some of the frustration that could be surrounding you at this time can be mitigated if you pursue the more creative side of your nature. Look at all the opportunities around you and see if there isn't something that takes your fancy. As long as you are achieving something you can be happy – and it doesn't have to be practical.

31 WEDNESDAY   *Moon Age Day 4   Moon Sign Aquarius*

Affairs of the heart continue to be of paramount importance as the year draws to its close. Why not set today aside for enjoying yourself and for helping others to do the same? There is nothing remotely selfish about your nature at the moment, and you can keep the warm and sincere side of your personality to the fore.

RISING SIGNS FOR SCORPIO

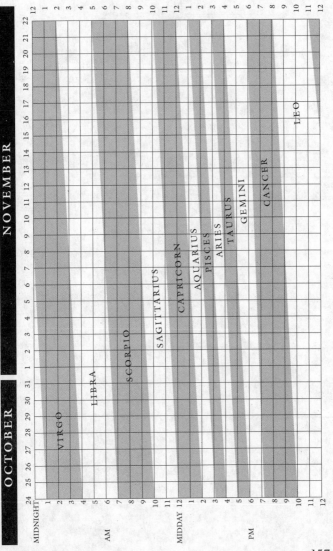

THE ZODIAC, PLANETS AND CORRESPONDENCES

The Earth revolves around the Sun once every calendar year, so when viewed from Earth the Sun appears in a different part of the sky as the year progresses. In astrology, these parts of the sky are divided into the signs of the zodiac and this means that the signs are organised in a circle. The circle begins with Aries and ends with Pisces.

Taking the zodiac sign as a starting point, astrologers then work with all the positions of planets, stars and many other factors to calculate horoscopes and birth charts and tell us what the stars have in store for us.

The table below shows the planets and Elements for each of the signs of the zodiac. Each sign belongs to one of the four Elements: Fire, Air, Earth or Water. Fire signs are creative and enthusiastic; Air signs are mentally active and thoughtful; Earth signs are constructive and practical; Water signs are emotional and have strong feelings.

It also shows the metals and gemstones associated with, or corresponding with, each sign. The correspondence is made when a metal or stone possesses properties that are held in common with a particular sign of the zodiac.

Finally, the table shows the opposite of each star sign – this is the opposite sign in the astrological circle.

Placed	Sign	Symbol	Element	Planet	Metal	Stone	Opposite
1	Aries	Ram	Fire	Mars	Iron	Bloodstone	Libra
2	Taurus	Bull	Earth	Venus	Copper	Sapphire	Scorpio
3	Gemini	Twins	Air	Mercury	Mercury	Tiger's Eye	Sagittarius
4	Cancer	Crab	Water	Moon	Silver	Pearl	Capricorn
5	Leo	Lion	Fire	Sun	Gold	Ruby	Aquarius
6	Virgo	Maiden	Earth	Mercury	Mercury	Sardonyx	Pisces
7	Libra	Scales	Air	Venus	Copper	Sapphire	Aries
8	Scorpio	Scorpion	Water	Pluto	Plutonium	Jasper	Taurus
9	Sagittarius	Archer	Fire	Jupiter	Tin	Topaz	Gemini
10	Capricorn	Goat	Earth	Saturn	Lead	Black Onyx	Cancer
11	Aquarius	Waterbearer	Air	Uranus	Uranium	Amethyst	Leo
12	Pisces	Fishes	Water	Neptune	Tin	Moonstone	Virgo